MW00514289

Library of Congress Cataloging-in-Publication Data
Mohamed, Mamdouh N.
    Hajj & 'Umrah: from A to Z
    Mamdouh N. Mohamed
    p. cm.
    Includes references.
    ISBN 0-915957-54-x
    1. Muslim pilgrims and pilgrimages —
        Islam - Islamic Pillars — Saudi Arabia-Mecca-
    Handbooks, manuals, etc. 1.Title.
    BP 187.3.M586 1995
    297'.55—dc20   95-42988   CIP
    Third Edition – 2005

Printed in the United States of America

10 9 8 7 6 5 4 3 2 1

Contents

Before Hajj Time	**A**
Types of Hajj	**B**
Before Traveling	**C**
Reach Miqat	**D**
Start Ihram	**E**
Go to Makkah	**F**
Make Tawaf	**G**
Make Sa'ee	**H**
End Ihram	**I**
Start Ihram	**J**
Stay in Mina	**K**
Attend 'Arafat	**L**
Stay in Muzdalifah	**M**
Jamrat al-'Aqabah	**N**
Slaughter a Sacrifice	**O**
Cut Your Hair	**P**
Make Tawaf	**Q**
Make Sa'ee	**R**
Stay in Mina	**S**
Throw Pebbles	**T**
Stay in Mina	**U**
Throw Pebbles	**V**
Stay in Mina	**W**
Throw Pebbles	**X**
Make Tawaf	**Y**
Back Home	**Z**

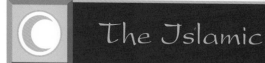

> ## "Pilgrimage is due on well-known months."
>
> **The Qur'an 2: 197**

Lunar months are either 29 or 30 days.

MUHARRAM

S	M	T	W	T	F	S
	1	2	3	4	5	6
7	8	9	10	11	12	13
14	15	16	17	18	19	20
21	22	23	24	25	26	27
28	29	30				

SAFAR

S	M	T	W	T	F	S
			1	2	3	4
5	6	7	8	9	10	11
12	13	14	15	16	17	18
19	20	21	22	23	24	25
26	27	28	29			

JUMADA AL-ULA

S	M	T	W	T	F	S
						1
2	3	4	5	6	7	8
9	10	11	12	13	14	15
16	17	18	19	20	21	22
23	24	25	26	27	28	29

JUMADA AL-AKHIRAH

S	M	T	W	T	F	S
1	2	3	4	5	6	7
8	9	10	11	12	13	14
15	16	17	18	19	20	21
22	23	24	25	26	27	28
29	30					

RAMADAN

S	M	T	W	T	F	S
					1	2
3	4	5	6	7	8	9
10	11	12	13	14	15	16
17	18	19	20	21	22	23
24	25	26	27	28	29	

SHAWWAL

S	M	T	W	T	F	S
						1
2	3	4	5	6	7	8
9	10	11	12	13	14	15
16	17	18	19	20	21	22
23	24	25	26	27	28	29

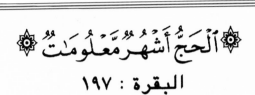

البقرة : ١٩٧

This calendar does not apply to a specific year.

RABI' AL-AWWAL

S	M	T	W	T	F	S
				1	2	3
4	5	6	7	8	9	10
11	12	13	14	15	16	17
18	19	20	21	22	23	24
25	26	27	28	29		

RABI' AL-AKHIR

S	M	T	W	T	F	S
					1	2
3	4	5	6	7	8	9
10	11	12	13	14	15	16
17	18	19	20	21	22	23
24	25	26	27	28	29	30

RAJAB

S	M	T	W	T	F	S
		1	2	3	4	5
6	7	8	9	10	11	12
13	14	15	16	17	18	19
20	21	22	23	24	25	26
27	28	29	30			

SHA'BAN

S	M	T	W	T	F	S
				1	2	3
4	5	6	7	8	9	10
11	12	13	14	15	16	17
18	19	20	21	22	23	24
25	26	27	28	29		

DHUL-QI'DAH

S	M	T	W	T	F	S
1	2	3	4	5	6	7
8	9	10	11	12	13	14
15	16	17	18	19	20	21
22	23	24	25	26	27	28
29	30					

DHUL-HIJJAH

S	M	T	W	T	F	S
		1	2	3	4	5
6	7	8	9	10	11	12
13	14	15	16	17	18	19
20	21	22	23	24	25	26
27	28	29				

Distances Between Ritual Places

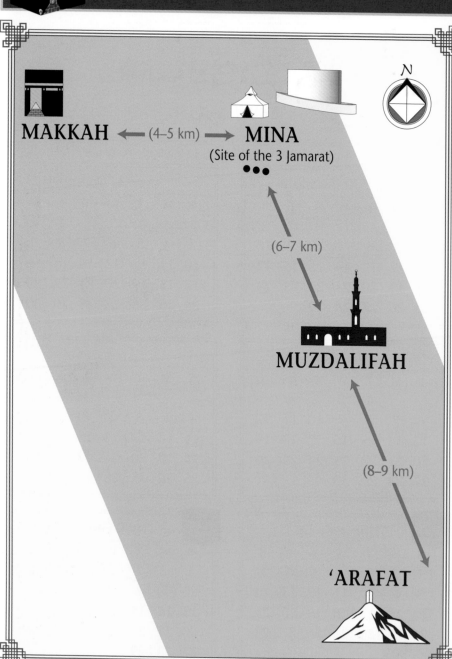

MAKKAH ← (4–5 km) → MINA
(Site of the 3 Jamarat)

(6–7 km)

MUZDALIFAH

(8–9 km)

'ARAFAT

N

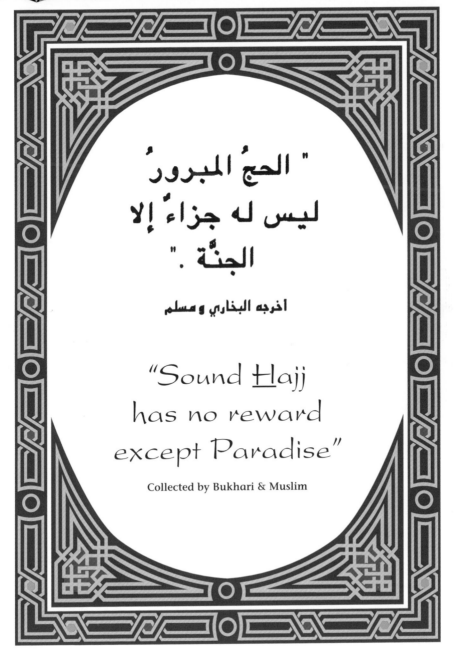

" الحجُ المبرورُ
ليس له جزاءً إلا
الجنَّة . "

أخرجه البخاري و مسلم

"Sound Ḥajj
has no reward
except Paradise"

Collected by Bukhari & Muslim

"Verily the first sanctuary appointed for mankind
was that at Bakkah, a blessed place, a guidance to the people."

The Qur'an 3: 96

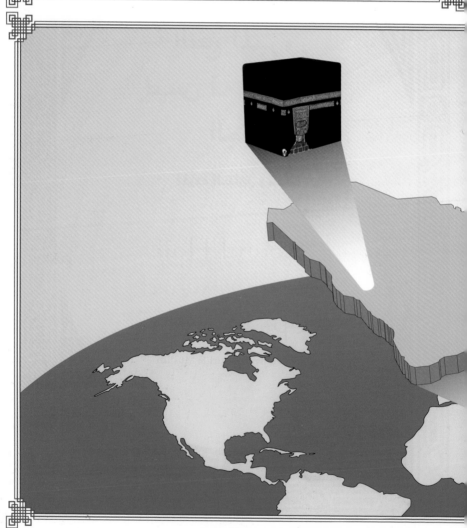

﴿۞ إِنَّ أَوَّلَ بَيْتٍ وُضِعَ لِلنَّاسِ لَلَّذِى بِبَكَّةَ مُبَارَكًا وَهُدًى لِّلْعَٰلَمِينَ ۞﴾

آل عمران : ٩٦

Introduction

In the Name of Allah, the Most Merciful, the Most Gracious.

All praise to Almighty Allah,
Who guided me to bring this project to completion.

A pilot study was conducted, in addition to extensive observation of pilgrims during seasons of Hajj. The study indicated that more than two-thirds of first time pilgrims could not perform the Hajj rituals in the correct manner. The representative sample showed that lack of correct knowledge, dearth of well-designed books, and unfamiliarity with the locations and ritual terms of Hajj, were among the main factors for occurrence of errors in Hajj. Thus, it was determined that first-time pilgrims are highly prone to commit mistakes, which for most people is a once-in-a-lifetime opportunity. This crucial fact prompted me to design a book that would lay out the rituals of Hajj in a step-by-step easy to follow format. Thus, the idea of a Hajj book, which could lay out the details from A to Z was born. Therefore the title "Hajj & 'Umrah from A to Z" seemed most appropriate.

The problem at hand of most pilgrims making mistakes in Hajj, warranted a careful study. As an instructional designer, I made a needs assessment of the situation and subsequently came up with design of an effective format to teach Muslims the rituals of Hajj. The result is an illustrated guide-book, which includes charts, diagrams and photographs. This book, God willing, will enable any Muslim to systematically learn the rituals of Hajj, and as a result perform their Hajj without any mistakes.

Besides laying out the details of Hajj in a simple format, another purpose of this book is to alleviate the tension, anxiety, and fear that some pilgrims may experience due to preconceived ideas about the difficulties of performing Hajj. Easy to follow and self-explanatory, this book makes sure that a pilgrim is aware of most common errors that occur at Hajj time. A pilgrim simply needs to follow the steps closely and accurately, to perform Hajj, in the correct manner, God willing.

The methodology I followed in this book is to trace the Sunnah of the Prophet Muhammad (peace be upon him) as illustrated by the famous Hadeeth collection by Imam Muslim and others of the "The Farewell Hajj of the Prophet" (pbuh). In so doing, I have kept this book far from the differences between the various schools of thought known as Madhahib.

The intended readers of this book include all English-speaking Muslims, who are ready to perform Hajj regardless of age, education or gender. Additionally, the book is designed to illustrate the Hajj Tamattu', as this type of Hajj includes all the steps required in the other two types of Hajj, namely Qiran and Ifrad. I have also included a chart under the title, "quick reference" that illustrates the similarities and differences between the three types of Hajj.

Finally, I would like to thank all those who supported me in writing, editing, and revising this book. Special thanks to Dr. Abdul-Haqq Hemmish. In particular I would like to express my thanks to those who kindly and patiently reviewed the Islamic content of this book many times, and those who provided me with pictures.

May Allah guide us all to the right path.

Dr. Mamdouh N. Mohamed
2006

How to use the Book

This booklet is designed primarily as a manual, a concept that may not be totally new to most people in our Islamic world. Briefly, it presents the material or the contents in a very sequential way to guarantee the fewest possible faults and errors.

Fortunately, when a person knows how to use this book/manual correctly and effectively, the outcome will be absolutely positive, if Allah is willing.

First,
> look carefully at the cover design to get acquainted with the steps and their sequences. Read through the book to get an overall, comprehensive idea of its contents. Whenever you find some new terms that you are not familiar with, consult the glossary at the end of the book.

Second,
> go to the quick-reference on the back cover where you will be able to see the similarities and differences among the three types of Hajj. Each type has a different color. Read this page carefully before you decide which one you will select.

Third,
> once you have made your selection, try to mark which steps are not applicable in Hajj Tamattu', the main focus of this book. This will help you skip the steps when the situation arises.

Fourth,
> follow each step accurately. Plan ahead by reading a couple of steps ahead of time. This is significant because when you start performing the rituals you will not have time to read thoroughly.

Fifth,
> always pay attention to the sequence of steps and the comments relating to them.

Sixth,
> the title "**Remember**" on each page is to remind you of the important things that many people often forget while they are performing the rituals. So pay close attention to them and try to abide by them, as they are very important.

Seventh,
> the "**Next Step**" subtitle is of vital importance, as it prepares you ahead of time for what you need before you actually start the following step.

Eighth,
> the title "**Warning**" is of vital significance, as it warns the pilgrims against:

> (a) some of the more common errors.

> (b) acts that nullify the Hajj.

> (c) acts that require a sacrifice or compensation.

Be assured that the book is very easy to follow and that it will guide you to perform your Hajj correctly if you abide by it.

Remember:
> Whenever in doubt, ask scholars before you act.
> This will save you **A LOT** of difficulties.

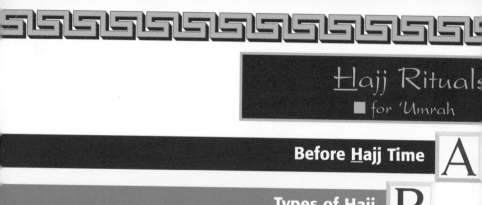

Hajj Rituals
■ for 'Umrah

Before Hajj Time A

Types of Hajj B

Before Traveling C

Reach Miqat D

Start Ihram E

Go to Makkah F

Make Tawaf G

Make Sa'ee H

End Ihram I

Start Ihram J

Stay in Mina K

Attend 'Arafat L

Stay in Muzdalifah M

Tamattu')
■ for 'Umrah

Z Back Home

Y Make Tawaf

X Throw Pebbles

W Stay in Mina

V Throw Pebbles

U Stay in Mina

T Throw Pebbles

S Stay in Mina

R Make Sa'ee

Q Make Tawaf

P Cut Your Hair

O Slaughter a Sacrifice

N Jamarat al-'Aqabah

MONEY:

Do not worry about exchanging money. You can do that very easily anywhere in Saudi Arabia.

SMALL GROUPS:

Close observation shows that people who move in large groups are subject to having either one or some of them lost, and/or missing some rituals or performing them late that may require them to compensate for that either by slaughtering an animal or by fasting or something else.

GOOD COMPANY:

Be sure to choose good company during your whole journey, because this helps you avoid arguments and helps you perform your Hajj correctly.

AVOID GETTING LOST:

It is recommended to arrange in advance with your group exactly where and when to meet and what to do in case of being late, and what to do if someone is lost. To help you, follow these procedures:

a. Arrange to meet at a very clear place where there is a clear, colored sign or landmark (e.g. the number of the gate of Al-Masjid Al-Haraam

b. Allow a specific range of time for those who come late for any reason, provided that this time does not affect the ritual to follow.

c. Be sure that everybody in your group is clearly notified.

FOOD:

a. Always avoid eating big meals, (a) because this is not healthy, and (b) this is not helpful for performing rituals.

b. The best foods to eat are fruits, and the best drinks are water and juice. They are everywhere and inexpensive.

c. Always put the remains of food in a plastic bag, and be sure to put it in a trash container.

MEDICATION:

Carry only indispensable medication that is essential for your health. Other common medicines can be obtained from any drugstore. You can get free first aid care everywhere.

PROTECTION:

Avoid being exposed to the sun for long periods of time. Always use umbrellas and drink a lot of liquids.

SERVICES FOR HANDICAPPED:

Special services are provided for the weak, the sick, the handicapped, and elderly people. Wheel chairs and on-shoulder-litters can be rented inside Al-Masjid Al-Haraam.

Errors to be Avoided

1. Ihraam	Missing the Ihram zone/area
2. Ihraam	Uncovering* the right shoulder in Ihraam. *Right shoulder should be done only during the 1st tawaaf.
3. Ihraam	Believing that there is a specific color for women's ihram.
4. Ihraam	Praying 2 rakaats after wearing Ihraam clothes.
5. Ihraam	Wearing pants or undergarment beneath the Ihraam clothes
6. Al-Masjid Al-Haraam	Kissing the ground of the masjid when entering it.
7. Al-Masjid Al-Haraam	Entering the masjid from a specific gate.
8. The Kaabah	Kissing, touching the Kabaah & Maqaam Ibrahim.
9. The Kaabah	Kissing the Yamani corner.
10. The Kaabah	Saying a specific dua' for every specific round.
11. The Kaabah	Uncovering the right shoulder during tawaaf.
12. The Kaabah	Trying to take anything from the Kaabah cover.
13. The Kaabah	Exiting the masjid backwardly after the final tawaaf.
14. Sa'ee area	Insisting on standing on the top of Safaa & Marwah
15. Sa'ee area	Doubling the walking between Safaa & Marwah. Walking between Safa & Marwah is considered one round
16. Shaving	Shaving part of the head and leaving the other for another Umrah
17. In Arafat	Not staying within Arafat Zone.
18. Muzdalefah	Insisting on collecting the pebbles from Muzdalefah.
19. Muzdalefah	Washing the pebbles before throwing the jamaraat.
20. Jamaarat	Throwing things other than pebbles (such as slippers)

Ḥajj

is the 5th pillar of Islam.
It is a once-in-a-lifetime
obligation upon male and female
sane adults who are eligible
(whose health and means permit).
In the words of the Qur'an

*"Pilgrimage to the House
is a duty unto Allah for mankind,
or him/her who can find
a way to perform it."*

The Qur'an 3: 97.

In carrying out this obligation,
Muslims fulfill Allah's call to Abraham:

*"And proclaim the pilgrimage
among humankind.
They come to you on foot
and on every animal
made lean by traveling
deep, distant ravines."*

The Qur'an 22: 27-28.

The Importance of Hajj

﴿ وَلِلَّهِ عَلَى ٱلنَّاسِ حِجُّ ٱلْبَيْتِ مَنِ ٱسْتَطَاعَ إِلَيْهِ سَبِيلًا ﴾

آل عمران : ٩٧

﴿ وَأَذِّن فِي ٱلنَّاسِ بِٱلْحَجِّ يَأْتُوكَ رِجَالًا وَعَلَىٰ كُلِّ ضَامِرٍ يَأْتِينَ مِن كُلِّ فَجٍّ عَمِيقٍ ﴾

الحج : ٢٧-٢٨

Valuable Pieces of Advice

"Pilgrimage is due on well-known months. So, whoever decides to make the pilgrimage, (let him/her remember that) there should be no obscenity or wickedness or angry argument on the pilgrimage."

The Qur'an 2: 197

Consciousness of Allah

Correct 'Aqidah

Repentance

Valuable Pieces of Advice

Pure Intention

Cleanliness

Correctness of Rituals

Mercy

Patience

Valuable Pieces of Advice

﷽ ٱلْحَجُّ أَشْهُرٌ مَّعْلُومَٰتٌ فَمَن فَرَضَ فِيهِنَّ ٱلْحَجَّ فَلَا رَفَثَ ﷽
﷽ وَلَا فُسُوقَ وَلَا جِدَالَ فِى ٱلْحَجِّ ﷽

البقرة : ١٩٧

Consciousness of Allah	Strive to please Allah by being conscious of the fact that He is All-Hearing and All-Seeing. Be conscious and fearful of Him in all your actions and speech.
Correct 'Aqidah	Every Muslim should be aware that his/her belief or Aqidah has to be correct for Hajj or any act of worship to be accepted by Him. Therefore, strive to always correct your belief by asking scholars who will provide you with proofs from the Quran and the Sunnah.
Pure Intention	A sincere intention for Hajj is of utmost importance. Allah only accepts that which is directed to Him alone.
Correctness of Rituals	Any ritual is only accepted if it is performed correctly, exactly as the Prophet Muhammad (pbuh) did it. "Whoever adds something new to our religion, it is rejected."
Patience	Part of the challenge of completing Hajj rituals is forgiveness and patience every pilgrim must exercise toward others.
Repentance	Do your best to make Hajj a repentance for all your sins. This repentance requires that you firmly resolve not to return back to any of these sins again, in addition to feeling remorse over them.
Mercy	Beautify your Hajj by being merciful to all. Do your best to help Muslims. Avoid pushing or hurting anyone in any of the Hajj rituals, especially Tawaf, Sa'ee, and the pebble throwing, as there are always large crowds there.
Cleanliness	Cleanliness is a true sign of faith. Therefore, strive to keep your heart, body, food, drink, and all other things clean. Also encourage others to keep ritual and worship places as clean as possible.

Daytime Temperatures and Humidity

"That (is the command). Whoever glorifies the commands of Allah, it surely is from the devotion of the hearts."

The Qur'an 22:32

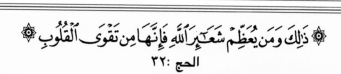

Month	Makkah Temperature Max. / Min.	Makkah Average Humidity	Madinah Temperature Max. / Min.	Madinah Average Humidity
January	27.4° / 17.5°	63%	22.7° / 10.5°	41%
February	27.5° / 17.6°	63%	27.0° / 12.0°	36%
March	31.0° / 20.6°	64%	30.2° / 17.3°	27%
April	34.5° / 21.2°	61%	35.1° / 21.0°	25%
May	35.0° / 24.3°	61%	39.2° / 23.7°	22%
June	37.5° / 25.4°	61%	42.3° / 27.4°	31%
July	39.0° / 26.7°	60%	42.4° / 27.9°	18%
August	39.2° / 28.3°	62%	42.5° / 28.7°	19%
September	35.9° / 26.9°	67%	41.2° / 27.3°	18%
October	35.0° / 24.4°	70%	36.5° / 21.5°	20%
November	33.0° / 22.0°	65%	30.0° / 16.0°	39%
December	28.9° / 20.2°	60%	24.1° / 12.5°	42%

Makkah

Makkah is located in western Saudi Arabia, about 80 km from the Red Sea.

It is part of the Hijaz mountains that are located in the southwest parallel to the Red Sea. It is very humid almost all year round.

Madinah

Madinah is located in northwestern Saudi Arabia, about 250 kilometers from the Red Sea. It is a rocky plateau. Its altitude above sea level is 620 meters. Its soil contains volcanic rocks especially in the west and the south-west coast. It is a barren land with a desert climate.

Items to Bring

Ihram Clothes

Sandals
(without a back) Not a boot

Personal Clothes

Umbrella

Money

Passport and Plane Ticket

Vaccination Card

Items Not to Bring

No Food

No Liquids

No Cigarettes or Tobacco

No Weapons

Hajj

Step by Step
(Tamattu')

Before Hajj Time	A
Types of Hajj	B
Before Traveling	C
Reach Miqat	D
Start Ihram	E
Go to Makkah	F
Make Tawaf	G
Make Sa'ee	H
End Ihram	I
Start Ihram	J
Stay in Mina	K
Attend 'Arafat	L
Stay in Muzdalifah	M
Jamrat al-'Aqabah	N
Slaughter a Sacrifice	O
Cut Your Hair	P
Make Tawaf	Q
Make Sa'ee	R
Stay in Mina	S
Throw Pebbles	T
Stay in Mina	U
Throw Pebbles	V
Stay in Mina	W
Throw Pebbles	X
Make Tawaf	Y
Back Home	Z

A Before Ḥajj

> "Surely Allah loves any of you who perfects his/her work."
> Collected by Al-Sayuti and accredited by Al-Albani.

PLACE: Homeland	**DATE:** No specific date
LOCATION: Wherever you live	**TIME:** No specific time

REMEMBER

THE MORE KNOWLEDGE YOU GET THE MORE SATISFYING YOUR ḤAJJ WILL BE.

SEQUENCE	COMMENTS

SEQUENCE

Step 1

◆ Make sure that you have a true and sincere intention of Ḥajj before you begin to make preparations.

Step 2

◆ Arrange enough legitimate funds for your journey and for your family.

Step 3

◆ Prepare yourself for good conduct throughout the whole journey.

Step 4

◆ Get adequate information about Ḥajj rituals and its fiqh.

　◆ Read some literature.

COMMENTS

◆ Pay all your debts.
◆ Redress all wrongs.
◆ Write your will.

◆ Always keep in mind the Hadith of Prophet Muhammad "Verily Allah is good, and He accepts only the good."

◆ Look for someone who can take care of your family whenever the need arises.

◆ Any woman should be accompanied by Maḥram.
◆ Check the pre-Ḥajj checklist accurately.

WARNING: *Be sure that the Ḥajj ritual is not accepted unless the money you obtained for it is acquired from a legitimate source.*

Before Ḥajj

"إنْ اللهَ يُحبُ إذا عملَ أحدُكم عملاً أنْ يتقنَهُ ".

أخرجه السيوطي وحسنه الألباني .

Pre-Ḥajj Checklist

	Yes	In Progress	No
1. Did you get your passport ready?	❏	❏	❏
2. Is it valid for 6 months?	❏	❏	❏
3. Have you applied for Ḥajj/'Umrah visa?	❏	❏	❏
4. Have you taken the required vaccination shots?	❏	❏	❏
5. Have you been informed about your sponsor (Mutawif)?	❏	❏	❏
6. Have you read some literature on Ḥajj/'Umrah?	❏	❏	❏
7. Have you paid all your debts?	❏	❏	❏
8. Have you bought the necessary Iḥram clothes?	❏	❏	❏
9. Have you prepared adequate funds for the journey?	❏	❏	❏
10. Have you confirmed your flights?	❏	❏	❏
11. Did you select the type of Ḥajj you intend to perform?	❏	❏	❏
12. Have you understood the basic Ḥajj terminology?	❏	❏	❏
13. Have you recited Talbiyah?	❏	❏	❏
14. Have you written your will?	❏	❏	❏
15. Did you leave enough money for your family?	❏	❏	❏
16. Did you chose somebody to take care of your family while you are away?	❏	❏	❏

NEXT STEP: The Types of Ḥajj —
It is important to think in advance which type of Ḥajj you want to perform.

"Whoever intends Ḥajj and 'Umrah together it is all right, and whoever intends to make Ḥajj it is all right, and whoever intends to make 'Umrah it is all right."

Collected by Bukhari & Muslim.

PLACE: Homeland	**DATE:** No specific date
LOCATION: Wherever you live	**TIME:** No specific time

REMEMBER

GET ENOUGH INFORMATION ABOUT THE DIFFERENT TYPES OF ḤAJJ.

SEQUENCE	COMMENTS

Step 1

◆ Be sure that you know the differences between the three types of Ḥajj.

(A) Tamattu':

◆ Making 'Umrah then Ḥajj in the same journey in the same year in the prescribed months of Ḥajj.

(B) Qiran:

◆ Making 'Umrah and Ḥajj at the same time in the same journey.

(C) Ifrad:

◆ Making Ḥajj only in the prescribed months of Ḥajj.

Step 2

◆ Be sure to select the exact type of Ḥajj you want to make.

WARNING: *Be sure that you know, if you select Tamattu' or Qiran, you must slaughter an animal, or fast 3 days during Ḥajj time and 7 days after going home.*

"فَمَنْ شاء أن يهلُّ بحجٍ وعمرةٍ فليهل ، ومن أراد أن يهلُّ
بحجٍ فليهل ، ومن أراد أن يهلُّ بعمرةٍ فليهل . "
أخرجه البخاري ومسلم .

The Three Types Hajj

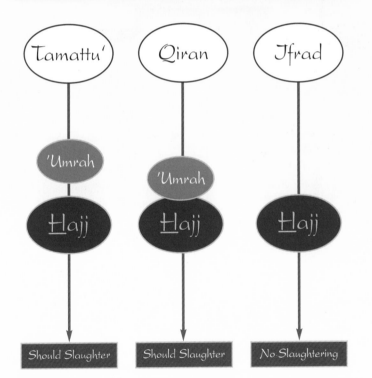

| Tamattu' | Qiran | Ifrad |

'Umrah

'Umrah

Hajj — Hajj — Hajj

| Should Slaughter | Should Slaughter | No Slaughtering |

NEXT STEP: Before Traveling —
It is time to redress all wrongs and start a new page in your life.
So, try to keep the new page as shining as possible.

C Before Traveling

> "Glorified be He Who has subdued these unto us, and we were not capable (of subduing them); And surely unto our Lord we are returning."
>
> **The Qur'an 43: 13-14**

PLACE: Homeland	**DATE:** The 3 months of Hajj
LOCATION: Wherever you live	**TIME:** No specific time

REMEMBER

DO THE RITUALS VERY ACCURATELY. YOU MAY NOT HAVE ANOTHER CHANCE.

SEQUENCE

Step 1
- If you are traveling by air or sea you have two options:
  - (a) put on Ihram before leaving
  - (b) put on Ihram on the flight/ship before passing over the Miqat

Step 2
- Before you take your flight or use any means of transportation, you should make a general cleanup getting ready for Ihram state:
  - Clipping nails, shaving underarm and pubic hair, and trimming mustache.
  - Take a shower and wash your body.
  - Get ready for putting on Ihram clothes.

COMMENTS

- If you decide to visit Madinah first, you will start Ihram on your way from Madinah to Makkah.
- Have Ihram clothes handy in your carry-on bag.

- Recommended

- Once you put on Ihram clothes, you have to observe Ihram obligations.
- Whatever the means of transportation you use, say the Qur'anic verse on the top of the next page.

WARNING: *Jeddah according to Sunnah is not Miqat. If you reach it without Ihram you should go to the nearest Miqat or slaughter an animal.*

﷽ سُبْحَنَ ٱلَّذِى سَخَّرَ لَنَا هَذَا وَمَا كُنَّا لَهُ مُقْرِنِينَ ﷽ وَإِنَّا إِلَى رَبِّنَا لَمُنقَلِبُونَ ﷽

الزخرف :١٣- ١٤

Talbiyah

It is time to learn Talbiyah. You will need it soon.

"Labbayk Allahumma Labbayk,
Labbayk la sharika laka Labbayk,
Innal hamda wanni'mata laka
walmulk
La sharika lak"

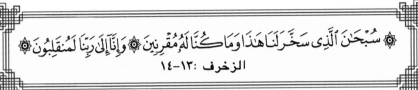

" لبَّيكَ اللهم لبَّيكَ ،
لبَّيكَ لا شريكَ لك لبَّيكَ ،
إنَّ الحمدَ والنعمةَ لك والملكَ ،
لاشريكَ لك . "

"O my Lord, Here I am at Your service,
Here I am.
There is no partner with You.
Here I am.
Truly, the praise and the provisions are Yours,
and so is the dominion and sovereignty.
There is no partner with you."

NEXT STEP: Reaching Miqat —
A pilgrim must put on Ihram clothes on reaching or before passing the Miqat.

D Reaching the Miqat

The Messenger (pbuh) specified these locations and said,
"They are the locations for whoever passes by them of those who are
not their inhabitants and for whoever wants to make Hajj and 'Umrah."

Collected by Bukhari & Muslim.

PLACE: One of the 5 Miqat points	**DATE:** The 3 months of Hajj
LOCATION: Saudi Arabia	**TIME:** No specific time

REMEMBER

DO NOT IMITATE PEOPLE BLINDLY; ALWAYS ASK SCHOLARS ABOUT ANY ISSUE.

SEQUENCE	COMMENTS
Step 1 ◆ When you reach the Miqat, make a whole body cleanup if you did not do so before leaving home.	◆ Recommended
Step 2 ◆ It is recommended to put on Ihram clothes after one of the 5 regular prayers.	
Step 3 ◆ Take off all your normal clothes. ◆ Put on the 2 clean, white seamless garments, and put on any sandals that do not reach your ankles, without any socks.	◆ Only men should take off their underwear. ◆ Women are required to wear clothing which meet the Islamic guidelines. This means covering the entire body except face and hands. Dress may be of any color as long as it is modest.

WARNING: *If you pass Miqat without Ihram you have to go back to the nearest Miqat to put on Ihram or you have to make a sacrifice.*

Reaching the Miqat

حدّد الرسولُ (صلى الله عليه وسلم) هذه المواقيتَ وقال" هنّ لهنّ ، لمن أتى عليهنّ من غير أهلهنّ ولمن أراد الحجّ والعمرةَ ."
أخرجه البخاري و مسلم .

The 5 Miqat Locations

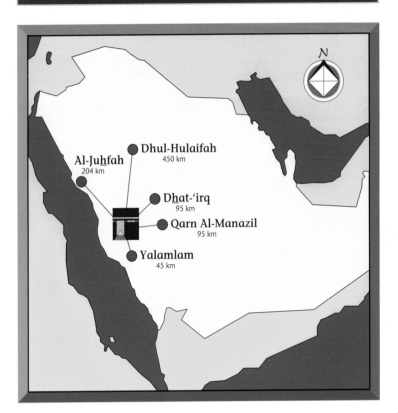

Dhul-Hulaifah
450 km

Al-Juhfah
204 km

Dhat-'irq
95 km

Qarn Al-Manazil
95 km

Yalamlam
45 km

NEXT STEP: Starting Ihram —
Get ready and be careful in observing the obligations of Ihram.

E Starting Ihram

> "Pilgrimage is due on well-known months. So, whoever decides
> to make the pilgrimage, (let him/her remember that) there should
> be no obscenity or wickedness or angry argument on the pilgrimage."
>
> **The Qur'an 2: 197**

PLACE: One of the 5 Miqat points	**DATE:** The 3 months of Hajj
LOCATION: Wherever you live	**TIME:** No specific time

REMEMBER

ONCE YOU ENTER IHRAM STATE, MAINTAIN RECITING THE TALBIYAH.

SEQUENCE	COMMENTS
Step 1	
◆ When you finish the regular prayer, say the intention of your selected type of Hajj:	◆ Men say the Talbiyah loudly while women say it to themselves, silently.
◆ If you intend to make Tamattu' say: (I am responding to You, my Lord, by 'Umrah with Tamattu' till Hajj.)	◆ Labbayk Allahumma 'Umrah mutamati'an biha 'ilal Hajj.
◆ If you intend to make Qiran say (I am responding to You, my Lord, by 'Umrah and Hajj together.)	◆ Labbayk Allahumma Hajj wa 'Umrah.
◆ If you intend to make Ifrad say (I am responding to You, my Lord, by Hajj.)	◆ Labbayk Allahumma Hajj.

WARNING: *If you do not follow the Ihram obligations accurately, you may need to redo your Hajj or make a sacrifice.*

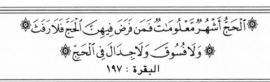

﴾ ٱلْحَجُّ أَشْهُرٌ مَّعْلُومَٰتٌ فَمَن فَرَضَ فِيهِنَّ ٱلْحَجَّ فَلَا رَفَثَ ﴿
﴾ وَلَا فُسُوقَ وَلَا جِدَالَ فِى ٱلْحَجِّ ﴿

البقرة : ١٩٧

Ihram Obligations

MEN	BOTH	WOMEN

MEN
2 Clean,
White Seamless
Garments
Izar & Rida

BOTH
Putting on Ihram

No Haircut or Shaving
No Clipping of Nails
No Perfumes or Colognes
No Scented Soap
No Killing or Hunting Animals
No Sexual Intercourse
No Marriage Proposals
No Marriage Contracts

WOMEN
Any modest,
dress covering
the body but
not the face
or the hands.

*Be careful, any sexual intercourse with one's spouse
nullifies the whole Hajj ritual.*

NEXT STEP: Going to Makkah —
*Once you reach Makkah, it is recommended to go directly
to Al-Masjid Al-Haraam.*

F Going to Makkah

> "O my Lord! Open to me the doors of Your Mercy."
>
> **Collected by Al-Tirmidhi, Ahmad, and Ibn Majah.**

PLACE: To Makkah	**DATE:** The 3 months of Hajj
LOCATION: Western Saudi Arabia	**TIME:** No specific time

REMEMBER

KEEP RECITING THE TALBIYAH UNTIL YOU REACH AL-MASJID AL-HARAAM.

SEQUENCE	COMMENTS
Step 1 ◆ When you make Ihram, it is preferable to go to Makkah directly.	◆ Recommended
Step 2 ◆ Go directly to al-Masjid al-Haraam.	◆ Recommended
Step 3 ◆ It is preferable to take a shower or make wudu' before going to al-Masjid al-Haraam.	◆ Recommended
Step 4 ◆ Enter the mosque from As-Salam gate. ◆ Say the above du'a'.	◆ Recommended

WARNING: *Menstruating women cannot make Tawaf until the period stops.*

Going to Makkah

"ربِّ افتح لي بابَ رحمتِكَ ."

أخرجه الترمذي وأحمد وابن ماجة.

Al-Masjid Al-Haraam

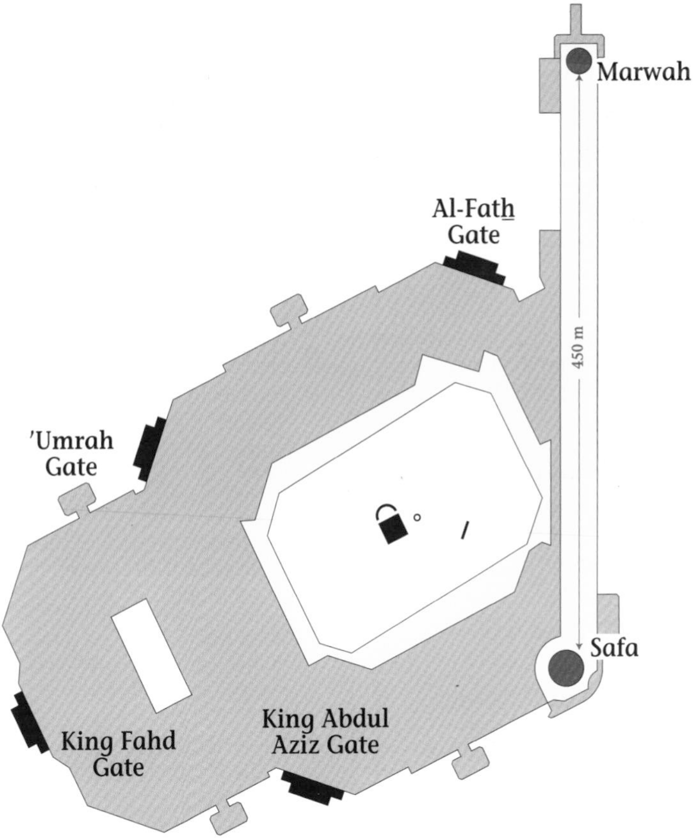

Marwah
Al-Fath
Gate
450 m
'Umrah
Gate
Safa
King Fahd
Gate
King Abdul
Aziz Gate

NEXT STEP: Making Tawaf —
Be merciful and helpful.
Do not push any pilgrim whatever the reason.

G Making Tawaf

> "Our Lord! Grant us goodness in this world and goodness in the Hereafter, and protect us from the torment of the fire!"
>
> **The Qur'an 2 : 201.**

PLACE: Around Ka'bah	DATE: The 3 months of <u>H</u>ajj
LOCATION: Al-Masjid al-<u>H</u>araam	TIME: No specific time

REMEMBER

A PRAYER IN THIS MOSQUE EQUALS ONE THOUSAND PRAYERS IN ANY OTHER MOSQUE.

SEQUENCE

Step 1
◆ Circle the Ka'bah 7 times.

  ◆ Start circling from the black stone by kissing or touching, or pointing to it, or raising your right hand while saying (Allahu Akbar) each time you come to it.

  ◆ While making tawaf, recite any du'a' or make Dhikr, then end each round at the black stone.

  ◆ Between Rukn Yamani and the black stone say this du'a': ⇨

Step 2
◆ When you finish the 7 rounds, pray 2 rak'at behind Maqam Ibrahim, if possible.

Step 3
◆ Drink from the water of Zamzam.

COMMENTS

Remember: To keep your right shoulder uncovered.

◆ The Ka'bah should be on the left hand.

◆ You can make Tawaf on any of the 3 floors; the ground, the first floor, or the roof.

◆ It is recommended for men only to increase their speed only in the first 3 rounds.

◆ *"Our Lord! Grant us goodness in this world and goodness in the Hereafter, and protect us from the torment of the fire!"*

◆ If it is not possible, pray anywhere in the mosque while facing the Ka'bah.

Remember: To cover right shoulder after Tawaf.

WARNING: *When you circle the Ka'bah do not go through <u>H</u>ijr Isma'il. Do not push any pilgrim whatever the reason.*

34

Making Tawaf

رَبَّنَآ ءَاتِنَا فِى ٱلدُّنْيَا حَسَنَةً وَفِى ٱلْأَخِرَةِ حَسَنَةً وَقِنَا عَذَابَ ٱلنَّارِ ۞

البقرة : ٢٠١

The Starting Point of Tawaf

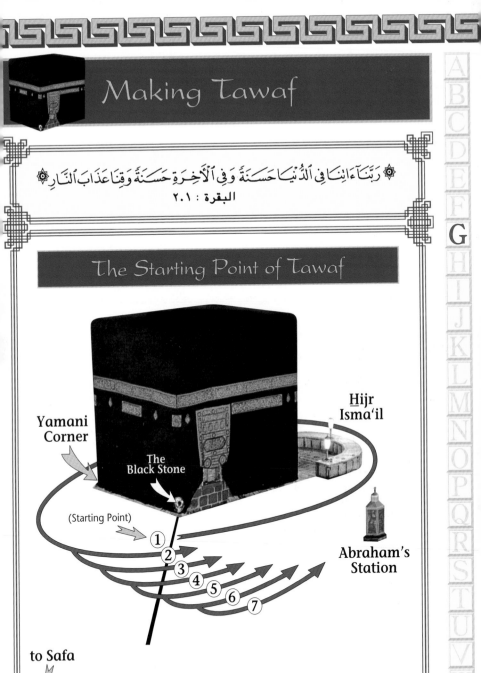

Yamani
Corner

Hijr
Isma'il

The
Black Stone

(Starting Point)

① ② ③ ④ ⑤ ⑥ ⑦

Abraham's
Station

to Safa

NEXT STEP: Making Sa'ee —
Start from Safa Hill. It should be on your right hand side.

H Making Sa'ee

> "Surely, Safa and Marwah are among the indications of Allah. So if those who make Hajj or make 'Umrah, should go around them, there is no sin in doing this. And if anyone volunteers to do good for himself, verily Allah recognizes and knows."
>
> **The Qur'an 2: 158**

PLACE: Between Safa & Marwah	**DATE:** The 3 months of Hajj
LOCATION: East of Ka'bah	**TIME:** After Tawaf

REMEMBER

THERE IS NO PARTICULAR DU'A' OR DHKIR FOR EACH ROUND.

SEQUENCE

Step 1
- Go to the Safa and Marwah area.
  - Praise Allah and make Takbeer 3 times, and make du'a'.

Step 2
- Descend from Safa and walk between the 2 hills (Safa and Marwah) at a normal speed.
  - Mention the name of Allah, recite Qur'an, and make du'a' while walking.
  - Ascend the hill of Marwah and make the same du'a' made at Safa or another du'a'.

Step 3
- Repeat steps 1 and 2 until you finish 7 rounds.
  - Make du'a' and praise Almighty Allah.

COMMENTS

Remember: To cover your right shoulder.

- From Safa to Marwah is counted as one round.
- Sa'ee should end at Marwah.
- Raise your hands and face the Ka'bah.
- Say the above Qur'anic verse on Safa then du'a'.
- Be very cautious whenever you descend and ascend the Safa and Marwah as it is very crowded.
- Only men should speed up their walk between the 2 green marked posts.
- Make du'a' for yourself, your family, and for all Muslims.

WARNING: *Menstruating women should not make Sa'ee until they are clean again.*

36

Making Sa'ee

﷽ إِنَّ ٱلصَّفَا وَٱلْمَرْوَةَ مِن شَعَآئِرِ ٱللَّهِ فَمَنْ حَجَّ ٱلْبَيْتَ أَوِ ٱعْتَمَرَ فَلَا جُنَاحَ عَلَيْهِ أَن يَطَّوَّفَ بِهِمَا ﷽
﷽ وَمَن تَطَوَّعَ خَيْرًا فَإِنَّ ٱللَّهَ شَاكِرٌ عَلِيمٌ ﷽

البقرة: ١٥٨

لا إلَهَ إلا الله وحده لا شريكَ له، له الملكُ وله الحمدُ ، يحيي ويميت وهو على كلِ شيءٍ قدير ،
لا إلَهَ إلا الله وحدَهُ، أَنْجَزَ وعدَهُ ، ونصرَ عبدَهُ ، وهزمَ الأحزابَ وحدَهُ

Sa'ee Area

The Fast-Walking Area
(Between the Green Columns)

MARWAH
(Finish)

SAFA
(Start)

⟵ 450 m ⟶

You can make Sa'ee from the 1st, 2nd or the 3rd floor.

NEXT STEP: Ending the State of Ihram —
Only those who selected Tamattu' will end their Ihram state.

I Ending 'Umrah and State of Ihram

> "Perform Hajj and 'Umrah for Allah."
> **The Qur'an 2: 196**

PLACE: Makkah	**DATE:** The 3 months of Hajj
LOCATION: Wherever you are	**TIME:** No specific time

REMEMBER

EVEN IF YOU END YOUR IHRAM STATE YOU SHOULD MAINTAIN GOOD CONDUCT.

SEQUENCE	COMMENTS
Step 1	
◆ End your 'Umrah.	◆ Only if you selected Tamattu' Hajj.
◆ After the 7th round, men should shave or trim all the hair on your head.	◆ The Sunnah of Prophet Muhammad (pbuh) is shaving the whole head. (Applicable for men only)
◆ Women are to cut only a finger tip's length from their hair.	
Step 2	
◆ Take off Ihram clothes and put on normal clothes.	◆ Until the 8th of Dhul-Hijjah.
◆ At this time, all the prohibitions of Ihram state are no longer applicable. You can resume your normal life.	

WARNING: *Do not cut your hair inside al-Masjid Al-Haraam. This is not the Sunnah. Always keep mosques clean.*

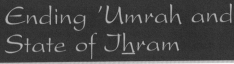

$$\textarabic{﴿ وَأَتِمُّوا الْحَجَّ وَالْعُمْرَةَ لِلَّهِ ﴾}$$

$$\textarabic{البقرة : ١٩٦}$$

Cutting/Shaving Mens Hair

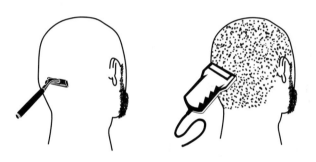

Cutting Womens Hair

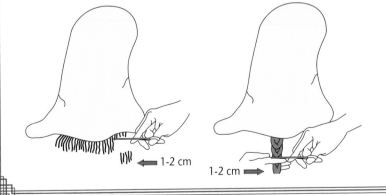

1-2 cm ⟵

1-2 cm ⟹

NEXT STEP: Starting Ihram of Hajj —
Try to check how accurate your 'Umrah was before proceeding for Hajj.

Starting Ihram of Hajj

> "Pilgrimage is due on well-known months. So, whoever decides to make Pilgrimage, (let him remember that) there should be no obscenity nor wickedness or angry argument on the pilgrimage."
>
> **The Qur'an 2: 197**

PLACE: Saudi Arabia	**DATE:** 8th of Dhul-Hijjah
LOCATION: Wherever you are	**TIME:** Before noon

REMEMBER

THIS STEP IS ONLY FOR THOSE PILGRIMS WHO SELECTED TAMATTU'.

SEQUENCE	COMMENTS
Step 1 ◆ Take a shower or make wudu' before you put on Ihram clothes.	◆ (The Day of Tarwiyah).
Step 2 ◆ Put on Ihram and pray 2 rak'at.	◆ From wherever you are.
Step 3 ◆ Only men say the intention loudly: (Labbayka Allahumma Hajjan) Meaning: (O Allah, I am responding to your call by making Hajj).	" لبّيكَ اللهم لبّيكَ ، لبّيكَ لا شريكَ لك لبّيكَ ، إنّ الحمدَ والنعمةَ لك والملكَ ، لاشريكَ لك . "
Step 4 ◆ Move to Mina before noon.	◆ Keep reciting the Talbiyah.

WARNING: *It is preferable for pilgrims to be in Mina before Dhuhr prayer.*

﴿ ٱلْحَجُّ أَشْهُرٌ مَّعْلُومَاتٌ فَمَن فَرَضَ فِيهِنَّ ٱلْحَجَّ فَلَا رَفَثَ ﴾
﴿ وَلَا فُسُوقَ وَلَا جِدَالَ فِي ٱلْحَجِّ ﴾
البقرة : ١٩٧

Ihram Obligations

| MEN | BOTH | WOMEN |

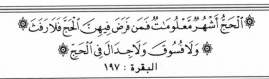

2 Clean, White Seamless Garments
Izar & Rida

Putting on Ihram

No Haircut or Shaving
No Clipping of Nails
No Perfumes or Colognes
No Scented Soap
No Killing or Hunting Animals
No Sexual Intercourse
No Marriage Proposals
No Marriage Contracts

Any modest, dress covering the body but not the face or the hands.

Be careful, any sexual intercourse with one's spouse or any action that leads to it nullifies the whole Hajj ritual.

NEXT STEP: Staying in Mina —
Maintain all the obligations of Ihram very accurately.

K   Staying in Mina

> *"That (is the command). Whoever glorifies the commands of Allah, it surely is from the devotion of the hearts."*
>
> **The Qur'an 22:32**

PLACE: Mina	**DATE:** 8th of Dhul-Hijjah
LOCATION: 5-6 km east of Makkah	**TIME:** Anytime before noon

REMEMBER

BE SURE THAT YOUR LOCATION IS INSIDE THE BOUNDARIES OF MINA.

SEQUENCE	COMMENTS
Step 1 ◆ Go to the area of Mina.	◆ The day of Tarwiyah
Step 2 ◆ Pray 5 daily prayers in Mina. Start with Dhuhr prayer.	◆ Shorten the 4-rak'at prayers to 2 rak'at only but do not combine prayers together.
Step 3 ◆ Stay in Mina until the sunrise of the 9th Dhul-Hijjah.	

WARNING: *If you do not attend 'Arafat or you leave it before Maghrib your whole Hajj is nullified, and you have to make a sacrifice.*

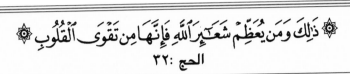

﷽ ذَلِكَ وَمَن يُعَظِّمْ شَعَائِرَ ٱللَّهِ فَإِنَّهَا مِن تَقْوَى ٱلْقُلُوبِ ﷽

الحج : ٣٢

Site of tents in Mina

NEXT STEP: Attending 'Arafat —
Do not get crowded on the mountain of Rahmah. You can stay in any place in 'Arafat. Be sure that your location is inside 'Arafat boundaries.

L Attending 'Arafat

> "There is no god but Almighty Allah, there is no partner with Him.
> He has the Sovereignty and He deserves all praises.
> He is Almighty Allah Who is capable of doing everything."
>
> **Collected by Al-Tirmidzi.**

PLACE: 'Arafat	**DATE:** 9th of Dhul-Hijjah
LOCATION: 20 km southeast of Makkah	**TIME:** From sunrise to sunset

REMEMBER

BE SURE THAT YOU ARE WITHIN THE BOUNDARIES OF 'ARAFAT

SEQUENCE

Step 1
- ◆ Leave for 'Arafat.
  - ◆ Keep reciting the Talbiyah.

Step 2
- ◆ Stay in 'Arafat.
  - ◆ Listen to the Khutbah at Masjid Namira (if possible) then pray Dhuhr and 'Asr at noon.
  - ◆ Spend the whole day praising Allah and glorifying Him.
  - ◆ Ask Allah for forgiveness and guidance.
  - ◆ Make repentance.
  - ◆ Make du'a' for Muslims.

Step 3
- ◆ After sunset, leave for Muzdalifah.
  - ◆ Move quietly while reciting the Talbiyah.

COMMENTS

- ◆ 'Arafat Day

- ◆ Shorten and combine them.

- ◆ Though it is recommended to be on the mountain of Rahmah, it is not necessary as it is crowded.

- ◆ Always repeat the above du'a'. (Hadith)

- ◆ Just after sunset

WARNING: *THIS IS THE MOST IMPORTANT RITUAL OF HAJJ.*
If you leave before Maghrib your whole Hajj is nullified, and you have to make a sacrifice.

Attending 'Arafat

" لا إلهَ إلا الله وحدَهُ لا شريك لَه ، له الملكُ وله الحمدُ ،
وهو على كل شيءٍ قدير . "
أخرجه الإمام الترمذي .

The Mount of Rahmah

*It is **NOT** necessary to be on the mountain.

NEXT STEP: Staying the night in Muzdalifah —
Stay the whole night until sunrise next day.

45

M Staying the Night in Muzdalifah

> "When you pass over the mountain of 'Arafat, remember Almighty Allah by the sacred spot."
>
> **The Qur'an 2: 198**

PLACE: Muzdalifah	**DATE:** 9th of Dhul-Hijjah
LOCATION: 8-9 km north of 'Arafat	**TIME:** From sunset to sunrise

REMEMBER

YOU CAN PICK UP THE 7 PEBBLES FOR JAMARAT AL-AQABAH

SEQUENCE	COMMENTS
Step 1 ◆ Leave for Muzdalifah quietly.	
Step 2 ◆ Stay the night in Muzdalifah.	
◆ Once you reach Muzdalifah, pray Maghrib and 'Isha' there.	◆ Combine the 2 prayers. Shorten 'Isha' prayer to 2 rak'at.
◆ Pray Fajr there.	
◆ Go to al-Mash'ar al-Haraam and make du'a' until the brightness of the sun is widespread.	
Step 3 ◆ Leave Muzdalifah for Mina.	◆ Speed up your walk when you pass by Muhasir valley.
◆ Mention the name of Allah, and recite the Talbiyah until you stone Jamrat al-'Aqabah.	

WARNING: *No one should leave Muzdalifah before Fajr without a legitimate excuse; only women, the old, and the weak.*

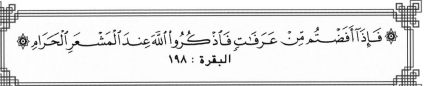

﴿ فَإِذَآ أَفَضْتُم مِّنْ عَرَفَـٰتٍ فَٱذْكُرُوا۟ ٱللَّهَ عِندَ ٱلْمَشْعَرِ ٱلْحَرَامِ ﴾

البقرة : ١٩٨

1-1¹/₂ cm

*You can take the pebbles from Mina as well.

NEXT STEP: Throwing stones at Jamrat al-'Aqabah —
Carry more pebbles than needed to avoid losing or misthrowing some of them.

Throwing Pebbles at Jamrat al-'Aqabah

> "That (is the command). Whoever glorifies the commands of Allah, it surely is from the devotion of the hearts."
>
> **The Qur'an 22:32**

PLACE: Jamarat Area	DATE: The 10th of Dhul-Hijjah
LOCATION: Southwestern Mina	TIME: After sunrise

REMEMBER

ALWAYS BE CALM, AVOID PUSHING PEOPLE, AND PERFORM THE RITUALS CORRECTLY.

SEQUENCE

Step 1
- Reaching Mina.
  - When you reach Mina, go to Jamrat al-'Aqabah (Al-kubra)

Step 2
- Throw 7 pebbles successively.
  - Throw while making Takbeer with each one.

COMMENTS

- The feast day ('Eid Day)
- It is the closest Jamrah to Makkah

- The size of the pebble should not exceed that of a bean.
- Weak and sick people can appoint others to throw stones on behalf of them.
- You can throw pebbles either from under the Jamarat bridge or above it

WARNING: *Be sure the pebbles touch the inside of the Jamrah fence.*

۞ ذَلِكَ وَمَن يُعَظِّمْ شَعَـٰئِرَ اللَّهِ فَإِنَّهَا مِن تَقْوَى الْقُلُوبِ ۞
الحج: ٣٢

Jamarat Area

to Makkah

③
Al-'Aqabah
(Large)

About
190 m

②
Al-Wusta
(Medium)

About
150 m

①
Al-Sughra
(Small)

N

to 'Arafat

NEXT STEP: Slaughtering / Cutting Hair / Tawaf Ifadah —
These 3 rituals alternate. You can begin with any of them.

O Slaughtering a Sacrifice

> "And for every nation have We appointed a ritual,
> that they may mention the name of Allah over the beast of cattle
> that He has given them for food."
>
> **The Qur'an 22:34**

PLACE: Mina	**DATE:** From 10th until 13th Dhul-Hijjah
LOCATION: 6-7 km east of Makkah	**TIME:** After sunrise of the 10th

REMEMBER

IF YOU SELECT IFRAD, YOU DO NOT NEED TO SACRIFICE, UNLESS YOU VOLUNTEER.

SEQUENCE

Step 1
- Slaughter the sacrifice.
  - After finishing the throwing, go to slaughter the sacrifice.
  - Be sure that it is a sheep, or $1/7$ share of a cow or a camel, and share it with other people.
  - You have the option to start with any of the following rituals:
    - slaughtering
    - cutting your hair
    - making Tawaf Ifadah

COMMENTS

- The feast day (The 'Eid Day)
- Always choose the best animal and avoid those with defects.
- You can slaughter the animal yourself or by appointing someone to do it for you.
- You can eat up to $1/3$ of it, offer $1/3$ as a gift, and offer $1/3$ to the poor.
- Now you can pay the cost of the sacrifice and it will be slaughtered for you.

WARNING: *Be sure that you can slaughter any time during the four days; the 10th, the 11th, the 12th, and the 13th, but not after that.*

Slaughtering a Sacrifice

وَلِكُلِّ أُمَّةٍ جَعَلْنَا مَنسَكًا لِّيَذْكُرُوا اسْمَ اللَّهِ عَلَىٰ مَا رَزَقَهُم مِّن بَهِيمَةِ الْأَنْعَامِ ۗ

الحج : ٣٤

Types of Sacrifice

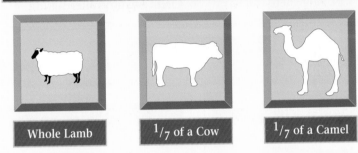

| Whole Lamb | $1/7$ of a Cow | $1/7$ of a Camel |

Dividing Your Sacrifice

$1/3$ Charity $1/3$ Gift $1/3$ Yourself

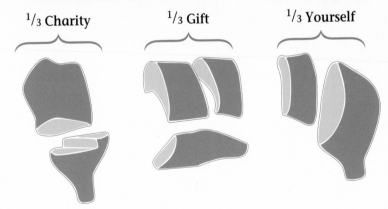

NEXT STEP: Cutting Hair —
Try to keep the ritual places as clean as possible.

P Cutting Hair

> "And shave not your heads until the gifts
> (the slaughtered animals) have reached their destination."
>
> **The Qur'an 2: 196**

PLACE: Mina/Makkah	**DATE:** 10th of Dhul-Hijjah
LOCATION: Anywhere	**TIME:** Anytime after sunrise

REMEMBER

THE SUNNAH OF PROPHET MUHAMMAD IS SHAVING THE HAIR ON THE HEAD.

SEQUENCE

Step 1

◆ Get your head shaved or trimmed. Start with the right side of the head. For women, trim only a finger tip's length from the hair.

Step 2

◆ After cutting your hair, you have reached (at-tahalul al-asghar) the partial ending of Ihram.

   ◆ At this phase, all the prohibitions of Ihram state are no longer applicable. A pilgrim can resume normal life except for sexual intercourse.

COMMENTS

◆ Always keep the ritual places as clean as possible.

◆ The total ending of Ihram state (at-tahalul al-akbar) will be after finishing the Tawaf and Sa'ee.

WARNING: *Be sure that the prohibitions of Ihram state are lifted except sexual intercourse with one's spouse.*

Cutting Hair

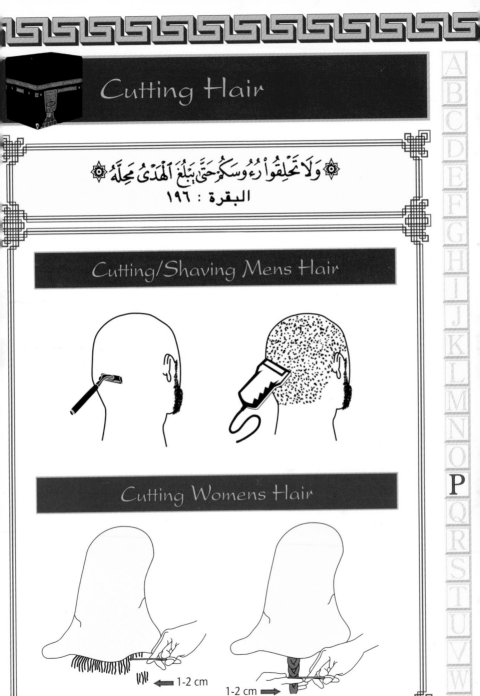

﷽ وَلَا تَحْلِقُوا رُءُوسَكُمْ حَتَّىٰ يَبْلُغَ ٱلْهَدْىُ مَحِلَّهُۥ ﷽

البقرة : ١٩٦

Cutting/Shaving Mens Hair

Cutting Womens Hair

1-2 cm ←

1-2 cm →

NEXT STEP: Making Tawaf Ifadah —
*It is usually very crowded, so be patient and calm
and help others.*

Q Making Tawaf Ifadah

> "And let them go around the ancient House (The Ka'bah)."
> **The Qur'an 22: 29**

PLACE: Around Ka'bah	**DATE:** 10th of Dhul-Hijjah
LOCATION: Al-Masjid Al-Haraam	**TIME:** Anytime after sunrise

REMEMBER

YOU HAVE THE OPTION TO POSTPONE TAWAF IFADAH TO A LATER TIME.

SEQUENCE

Step 1
◆ Circle the Ka'bah 7 times.

  ◆ Start circling from the black stone by kissing or touching, or pointing to it, or raising your right hand while saying (Allahu Akbar) each time you come to it.

  ◆ While making tawaf, recite any du'a' or make Dhikr, then end each round at the black stone.

  ◆ Between Rukn Yamani and the black stone say this du'a':⇨

Step 2
◆ When you finish the 7 rounds, pray 2 rak'at behind Maqam Ibrahim, if possible.

COMMENTS

◆ It is recommended that men have their right shoulders not covered by Ihram clothes.

◆ It is only recommended for men to increase their speed only in the first 3 rounds.

◆ *"Our Lord! Grant us goodness in this world and goodness in the Hereafter, and protect us from the torment of the fire!"*

◆ If it is not possible to pray behind Maqam Ibrahim, pray anywhere in the mosque while facing the Ka'bah.

WARNING: *Menstruating women should not make Tawaf until their period stops. Sa'ee can be postponed until they are clean again.*

Making Tawaf

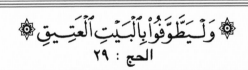

وَلْيَطَّوَّفُواْ بِالْبَيْتِ ٱلْعَتِيقِ

الحج : ٢٩

The Starting Point of Tawaf

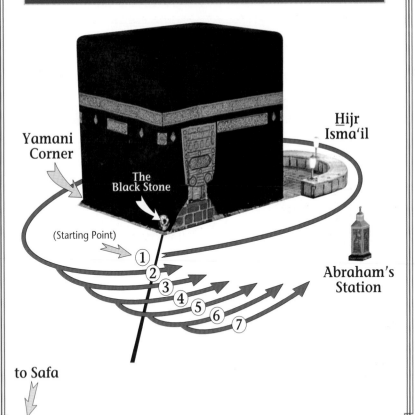

Yamani Corner

Ḥijr Ismaʻil

The Black Stone

(Starting Point)

① ② ③ ④ ⑤ ⑥ ⑦

Abraham's Station

to Safa

NEXT STEP: Making Saʻee —
If you select the Ifrad or Qiran and already made Saʻee with the first Tawaf (visiting Tawaf), you do not need to make Saʻee again.

55

R Making Sa'ee

> "Surely, Safa and Marwah are among the indications of Allah.
> So if those who make Hajj or make 'Umrah, should go around them,
> there is no sin in doing this. And if anyone volunteers to do good for himself,
> verily Allah recognizes and knows."
>
> **The Qur'an 2: 158**

PLACE: Between Safa & Marwah	**DATE:** 10th of Dhul-Hijjah
LOCATION: Al-Masjid Al-Haraam	**TIME:** After making Tawaf

REMEMBER

WHENEVER YOU MAKE TAWAF IFADAH, YOU CAN FOLLOW IT WITH SA'EE.

SEQUENCE

Step 1
◆ Go to the Safa and Marwah area.
  ◆ Praise Allah and make Takbeer 3 times, and make du'a'.

Step 2
◆ Descend from Safa and walk between the 2 hills (Safa and Marwah) at a normal speed.
  ◆ Mention the name of Allah, recite Qur'an, and make du'a' while walking.
  ◆ Ascend the hill of Marwah and make the same du'a' made at Safa or another du'a'.

Step 3
◆ Repeat steps 1 and 2 until you finish 7 rounds.
  ◆ Make du'a' and praise Almighty Allah.

COMMENTS

◆ From Safa to Marwah is counted as one round.

◆ Sa'ee should end at Marwah.

◆ Raise your hands and face the Ka'bah.

◆ Say the above Qur'anic verse on Safa then du'a'.

◆ Be very cautious whenever you descend and ascend the Safa and Marwah as it is very crowded.

◆ Only men should speed up their walk between the 2 green marked posts.

◆ Make du'a' for yourself, your family, and for all Muslims.

WARNING: *Menstruating women should not make Sa'ee until they are clean.*

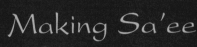

Making Sa'ee

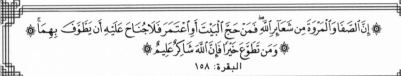

لا إلهَ إلا اللهُ وحدهُ لا شريكَ له، له الملكُ وله الحمدُ ، يحيي ويميت وهو على كلِ شيءٍ قديرٌ ،
لا إلهَ إلا اللهُ وحدهُ، أنجزَ وعدَهُ ، ونصرَ عبدَهُ ، وهزمَ الأحزابَ وحدهُ

Sa'ee Area

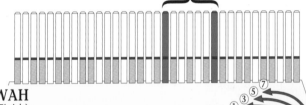

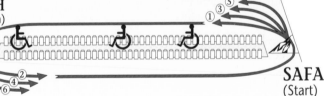

You can make Sa'ee from the 1st, 2nd or the 3rd floor.

NEXT STEP: *Staying in Mina —*
*Try to benefit from scholars by attending their lectures and
asking them questions that you need to know.*

57

S Staying in Mina

> *"And remember Allah through the appointed days."*
> **The Qur'an 2: 203**

PLACE: Mina	**DATE:** 10th of Dhul-Hijjah
LOCATION: 5-6 km east of Makkah	**TIME:** Most of the night

REMEMBER

IT IS A GOOD OPPORTUNITY TO GET A LOT OF KNOWLEDGE FROM SCHOLARS.

SEQUENCE	COMMENTS
Step 1	
◆ Leave Makkah for Mina.	
◆ After finishing your Tawaf and Sa'ee, go to spend the night in Mina.	
Step 2	
◆ Stay in Mina.	◆ Shorten the 4-rak'at to 2 rak'at.
◆ Pray the daily and night prayers in Mina.	◆ Do not combine prayers together.

WARNING: *The minimum stay in Mina should exceed most of the night. Otherwise you are required to make a sacrifice.*

Staying in Mina

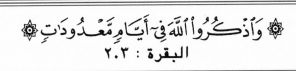

﷽ وَٱذْكُرُواْ ٱللَّهَ فِي أَيَّامٍ مَّعْدُودَاتٍ ﷽

البقرة : ٢٠٣

Site of the tents in Mina

NEXT STEP: Throwing pebbles at the 3 Jamarat.
Get your pebbles ready.

T Throwing Pebbles at the 3 Jamarat

> "That (is the command). Whoever glorifies the commands of Allah, it surely is from the devotion of the hearts."
>
> **The Qur'an 22:32**

PLACE: Jamarat area	**DATE:** 11th of Dhul-Hijjah
LOCATION: Southwestern Mina	**TIME:** After Dhuhr prayer

REMEMBER

BE SURE THAT YOU THROW AFTER DHUHR PRAYER.

SEQUENCE	COMMENTS

Step 1
 ◆ Go to Jamarat area in Mina.
    ◆ Start with al-Jamrah as-Sughra. (The smallest)
    ◆ Start throwing the 7 pebbles successively while making Takbeer with each pebble. Distance yourself and make du'a'.
	◆ The size of the pebble should not exceed that of a bean.

Step 2 ◆ Go to al-Jamrah al-Wusta (Medium) ◆ Start throwing the 7 pebbles successively while making Takbeer with each pebble. Distance yourself and make du'a'.	
Step 3 ◆ Go to al-Jamrah al-Kubra. (The Largest) ◆ Start throwing the 7 pebbles successively while making Takbeer with each pebble.	◆ Without making du'a'.

WARNING: *You should stay at least from midnight to Fajr in Mina.*

Throwing Pebbles at the 3 Jamarat

﴿ ذَٰلِكَ وَمَن يُعَظِّمْ شَعَـٰئِرَ ٱللَّهِ فَإِنَّهَا مِن تَقْوَى ٱلْقُلُوبِ ﴾

الحج: ٣٢

Jamarat Area

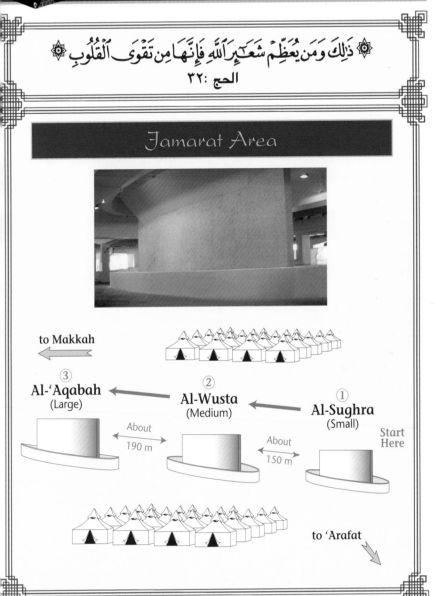

to Makkah ←

③ **Al-'Aqabah** (Large)

② **Al-Wusta** (Medium)

① **Al-Sughra** (Small)

Start Here

About 190 m

About 150 m

to 'Arafat

NEXT STEP: Staying in Mina —
Maintain good conduct. Keep Mina as clean as possible

U Staying in Mina

> "And remember Allah through the appointed days."
>
> **The Qur'an 2: 203**

PLACE: Mina	**DATE:** 11th of Dhul-Hijjah
LOCATION: 5-6 km east of Makkah	**TIME:** At least from midnight to Fajr

REMEMBER

IF YOU INTEND TO STAY ONLY 2 DAYS, YOU MUST LEAVE MINA BEFORE MAGHRIB.

SEQUENCE	COMMENTS
Step 1	
◆ Leave Makkah for Mina.	
◆ After finishing your Tawaf and Sa'ee, go to spend the night in Mina.	
Step 2	
◆ Stay in Mina.	◆ Shorten the 4-rak'at to 2 rak'at.
◆ Pray the daily and night prayers in Mina.	◆ Do not combine prayers together.

WARNING: *The minimum stay in Mina is from midnight until sunrise. Otherwise you are required to make a sacrifice.*

Staying in Mina

﷽ وَٱذۡكُرُواْ ٱللَّهَ فِىٓ أَيَّامٍ مَّعۡدُودَٰتٍۚ ﷽

البقرة : ٢٠٣

NEXT STEP: *Throwing pebbles at the 3 Jamarat.*
Get your pebbles ready. Pick them from Mina.

> "Whoever hastens (departure) by two days, it is no sin for him,
> and whoever delays, it is no sin for whoever wants to avoid error.
> Be careful of your duty to Allah, and know
> that unto Him you will be gathered."
>
> **The Qur'an 2: 203**

PLACE: Jamarat area	**DATE:** 12th of Dhul-Hijjah
LOCATION: Southwestern Mina	**TIME:** After Dhuhr prayer

REMEMBER

IT IS ALWAYS CROWED IN THE JAMARAT AREA. DO NOT PUSH ANY PILGRIM.

SEQUENCE	COMMENTS
Step 1	
◆ Go to Jamarat area in Mina.	
◆ Start with al-Jamrah as-Sughra. (The smallest)	
◆ Start throwing the 7 pebbles successively while making Takbeer with each pebble. Distance yourself and make du'a'.	◆ The size of the pebble should not exceed that of a bean.
Step 2	
◆ Go to al-Jamrah al-Wusta (Medium)	
◆ Start throwing the 7 pebbles successively while making Takbeer with each pebble. Distance yourself and make du'a'.	
Step 3	
◆ Go to al-Jamrah al-Kubra. (The Largest)	
◆ Start throwing the 7 pebbles successively while making Takbeer with each pebble.	◆ Without making du'a'.

WARNING: *If you decide to stay only 2 days, you have to leave Mina before Maghrib.*

Throwing Pebbles at the 3 Jamarat

﴿ وَاذْكُرُوا اللَّهَ فِي أَيَّامٍ مَّعْدُودَاتٍ فَمَن تَعَجَّلَ فِي يَوْمَيْنِ فَلَا إِثْمَ عَلَيْهِ وَمَن تَأَخَّرَ فَلَا إِثْمَ عَلَيْهِ لِمَنِ اتَّقَىٰ ﴾ ﴿ وَاتَّقُوا اللَّهَ وَاعْلَمُوا أَنَّكُمْ إِلَيْهِ تُحْشَرُونَ ﴾

البقرة : ٢٠٣

Jamarat Area

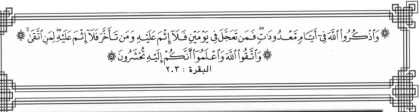

to Makkah

③ **Al-'Aqabah** (Large)

② **Al-Wusta** (Medium)

① **Al-Sughra** (Small)

Start Here

 About 190 m

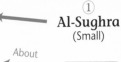 About 150 m

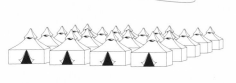

to 'Arafat

NEXT STEP: Staying in Mina —
Get ready to buy Islamic books for your library and for your friends.

W Staying in Mina

> "And remember Allah through the appointed days."
>
> **The Qur'an 2: 203**

PLACE: Mina	**DATE:** 12th of Dhul-Hijjah
LOCATION: 5-6 km east of Makkah	**TIME:** At least from midnight to Fajr

REMEMBER

IT IS A GOOD OPPORTUNITY TO GET ACQUAINTED WITH MUSLIMS FROM ALL OVER THE WORLD.

SEQUENCE

Step 1

◆ Leave Makkah for Mina.

   ◆ After finishing your Tawaf and Sa'ee, go to spend the night in Mina.

Step 2

◆ Stay in Mina.

   ◆ Pray the daily and night prayers in Mina.

COMMENTS

◆ Shorten the 4-rak'at to 2 rak'at.

◆ Do not combine prayers together.

WARNING: *Spend most of the night in Mina. Otherwise you are required to make a sacrifice.*

۞ وَاذْكُرُواْ اللَّهَ فِي أَيَّامٍ مَّعْدُودَاتٍ ۞

البقرة : ٢٠٣

Site of the tents in Mina

NEXT STEP: Throw pebbles at the 3 Jamarat —
Get your pebbles ready.

X Throwing Pebbles at the 3 Jamarat

> "That (is the command). Whoever glorifies the commands of Allah, it surely is from the devotion of the hearts."
>
> **The Qur'an 22:32**

PLACE: Jamarat area	**DATE:** 13th of Dhul-Hijjah
LOCATION: Southwestern Mina	**TIME:** After Dhuhr prayer

REMEMBER

IT IS ALWAYS CROWDED IN THE JAMARAT AREA. DO NOT PUSH ANY PILGRIM.

SEQUENCE	COMMENTS
Step 1 ◆ Go to Jamarat area in Mina. 　◆ Start with al-Jamrah as-Sughra. (The smallest) 　◆ Start throwing the 7 pebbles successively while making Takbeer with each pebble. Distance yourself and make du'a'.	◆ The size of the pebble should not exceed that of a bean.
Step 2 ◆ Go to al-Jamrah al-Wusta (Medium) 　◆ Start throwing the 7 pebbles successively while making Takbeer with each pebble. Distance yourself and make du'a'.	
Step 3 ◆ Go to al-Jamrah al-Kubra. (The Largest) 　◆ Start throwing the 7 pebbles successively while making Takbeer with each pebble.	◆ Without making du'a'.

WARNING: *Do not forget to throw the pebbles inside the fence of each Jamarat.*

ذَٰلِكَ وَمَن يُعَظِّمْ شَعَائِرَ اللَّهِ فَإِنَّهَا مِن تَقْوَى الْقُلُوبِ

الحج: ٣٢

Jamarat Area

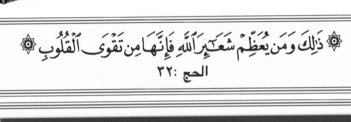

to Makkah

③ **Al-'Aqabah** (Large)

About 190 m

② **Al-Wusta** (Medium)

About 150 m

① **Al-Sughra** (Small)

Start Here

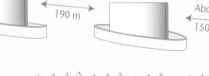

to 'Arafat

NEXT STEP: Making Tawaf (Farewell) —
Do not forget that you have to make Farewell Tawaf before you leave Makkah.

Y Making Tawaf (Farewell)

> " No one should leave (Makkah) unless his last step is visiting the House (making Tawaf)."
>
> **Collected by Muslim.**

PLACE: Al-Masjid Al-<u>H</u>araam	**DATE:** No specific date
LOCATION: Makkah	**TIME:** No specific time

REMEMBER

YOU SHOULD LEAVE MAKKAH DIRECTLY AFTER THE FAREWELL TAWAF.

SEQUENCE

Step 1
◆ Circle the Ka'bah 7 times.

- ◆ Start circling from the black stone by kissing or touching, or pointing to it, or raising your right hand while saying (Allahu Akbar) each time you come to it.

- ◆ While making tawaf, recite any du'a' or make Dhikr, then end each round at the black stone.

- ◆ Between Rukn Yamani and the black stone say this du'a':⟹

Step 2
◆ When you finish the 7 rounds, pray 2 rak'at behind Maqam Ibrahim, if possible.

COMMENTS

- ◆ **Remeber** that you are in regular clothes.

- ◆ It is recommended for men only to increase their speed only in the first 3 rounds.

- ◆ *"Our Lord! Grant us goodness in this world and goodness in the Hereafter, and protect us from the torment of the fire!"*

- ◆ If it is not possible to pray behind Maqam Ibrahim, pray anywhere in the mosque while facing the Ka'bah.

WARNING: *A menstruating woman can leave Makkah without making a Farewell Tawaf.*

Making Tawaf (Farewell)

The Starting Point of Tawaf

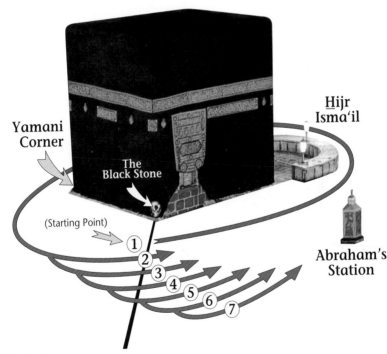

Yamani
Corner

The
Black Stone

Hijr
Isma'il

(Starting Point)

① ② ③ ④ ⑤ ⑥ ⑦

Abraham's
Station

to Safa

NEXT STEP: Back Home / Going to Madinah —
*Though it is neither obligatory nor related to Hajj, it is recommended for
a pilgrim to visit the mosque of Prophet Muhammad (pbuh) in Madinah.*

71

Z Back Home

> "There is no god but Almighty Allah, there is no partner with Him.
> He has the Sovereignty and He deserves all praises.
> He is Almighty Allah Who is capable of doing everything.
> We are returning, we are repenting, we are worshipping,
> we are prostrating to our Lord, we are grateful and thankful to Him.
> Surely Allah fulfilled His promise, and supported His followers,
> and defeated all parties alone."
>
> **Collected by Bukhari & Muslim.**

PLACE: To your homeland	**DATE:** Before your visa ends
LOCATION: Wherever you live	**TIME:** No specific time

REMEMBER

IF YOUR HAJJ IS ACCEPTED BY ALMIGHTY ALLAH, YOU LEAVE MAKKAH AS IF YOU HAD JUST BEEN BORN, WITHOUT ANY SIN, LIKE A BLANK WHITE PAPER.

SEQUENCE

Step 1

- Thank Allah who helped you perform Hajj.
- Ask Him to accept your rituals.
  - Promise Him to abide by His commands.

Step 2

- Pack up and go home safely.

COMMENTS

- "Whoever goes to Hajj without obscenity he or she will be forgiven as a new-born."

  Collected by Bukhari & Muslim

- "Sound Hajj has no reward except Paradise"

  Collected by Bukhari & Muslim

NEVER GO BACK AND COMMIT ANY SINS AGAIN.

Back Home

" لا إلهَ إلا الله وحدَهُ لا شريكَ له ، له المُلكُ وله الحمدُ ،
وهو على كلِ شيءٍ قديرُ ، أئبون تائبون ، عابدون ، ساجدون ،
لربِنا حامدون ، صدق اللهُ وعدَهُ ، ونصر عبدَهُ ، وهزم الأحزابَ وحدَهُ . "
أخرجه البخاري ومسلم .

Post-Hajj Checklist
(Self-Evaluation)

		1 2 3 4 5	
1.	To what extent has Hajj positively changed your life?	Low ☐☐☐☐☐	High
2.	To what extent have you realized the significance of Hajj?	Low ☐☐☐☐☐	High
3.	To what extent have you practiced unity with other Muslims?	Low ☐☐☐☐☐	High
4.	To what extent have you noticed equality among Muslims?	Low ☐☐☐☐☐	High
5.	To what extent have you made du'a' for all Muslims?	Low ☐☐☐☐☐	High
6.	To what extent has accurate Islamic knowledge been needed?	Low ☐☐☐☐☐	High
7.	To what extent have you felt the greatness of Islam?	Low ☐☐☐☐☐	High
8.	To what extent do you want to perform Hajj/'Umrah again?	Low ☐☐☐☐☐	High
9.	To what extent do Muslims need discipline in their lives?	Low ☐☐☐☐☐	High
10.	To what extent are you going to work actively for Islam?	Low ☐☐☐☐☐	High
11.	To what extent have you committed yourself to Islam?	Low ☐☐☐☐☐	High
12.	To what extent has Hajj corrected your faith (Aqidah)?	Low ☐☐☐☐☐	High
13.	To what extent did you buy Islamic books for your personal library and as gifts for other Muslims?	Low ☐☐☐☐☐	High
14.	Have you seriously repented for your past sins?	Low ☐☐☐☐☐	High

NEXT STEP: *Be a good dedicated Muslim who abides by correct Islam.*

Be sure you did not miss any of the Pillars of H̲ajj

Pillars of H̲ajj

1. Getting into the state of Ih̲ram with the Intention
2. Staying in Arafat
3. Making Tawaf
4. Making Sa'ee
5. Sleeping in Muzdalifah

Duties of H̲ajj

1. Sleeping in Muzdalifah and praying Fajr there.
2. Throwing the pebbles
3. Slaughtering an animal during H̲ajj
4. Shaving or cutting the hair of the head
5. Sleeping in Minah during the days of Tashriq
6. Farewell Tawaf

Visiting Madinah

A
B
C
D
E
F
G
H
I
J
K
L
M
N
O
P
Q
R
S
T
U
V
W
X
Y
Z

A — Visiting the Prophet's Mosque (pbuh)

> *"Any prayer in my mosque (The Prophet's Mosque) is better than one thousand prayers in any other mosque except al-Masjid al-Haraam (in Makkah)."*
>
> **Collected by the group except Abu Dawood.**

PLACE: Madinah	**DATE:** Any Time
LOCATION: 450 km Northeast of Makkah	**TIME:** Whenever you visit Madinah

REMEMBER

THOUGH THE VISIT IS NEITHER OBLIGATORY NOR PART OF HAJJ AT ALL, IT IS CONFIRMED SUNNAH

SEQUENCE

Step 1
- Enter the Prophet's Mosque.

Step 2
- Pray 2 rak'at as a greeting to the mosque.

Step 3
- Go to the Prophet's grave quietly and respectfully.

Step 4
- Make Salam to the Prophet (pubh) then his 2 companions, Abu-Bakr and 'Umar.
  - Leave the place and behave as if you are in other mosques.

COMMENTS

- Always have the intention of visiting the mosque and not the grave or the Prophet himself.

- It is recommended to pray in the Rawdah Area if possible because of the Hadith narrated by Bukhari and Muslim "Between my house and my pulpit is part of Paradise".

- Say O, Prophet, peace be upon you and Allah's mercy and blessing I bear witness that you carried the message to us, and fulfilled the responsibility in the best way, and advised the whole nation, and strived in the way of Allah to your maximum ability.

WARNING: *It is Shirk to circle around the grave or to face it and direct du'a' to the Prophet. It is un-Islamic to kiss the fence of the grave or touch it.*

"صلاةٌ في مسجدي هذا خيرٌ مِن ألفِ صلاةٍ فيما سواه
إلا المسجد الحرام ."

أخرجه الجماعة سوى أبي داوود.

The Prophet's Mosque (pbuh)

NEXT STEP: Visiting Masjid Quba' (optional)
*Get ready; clean yourself at home to pray 2 rak'at
at Masjid Quba'*

Z

Visiting Quba' Mosque

> "Whoever cleans up in his house, and comes to Quba' Mosque, and prays two rak'at (units of prayer) he will be given the reward for 'Umrah."
>
> **Collected by Tirmidhi.**

PLACE: Madinah	**DATE:** No specific date
LOCATION: Southern Madinah	**TIME:** No specific time

REMEMBER

THIS VISIT IS NOT PART OF HAJJ RITUALS. HOWEVER, IT IS STRONGLY RECOMMENDED TO PRAY THERE TWO RAK'AT.

SEQUENCE

Step 1

◆ Enter Quba' mosque from any gate.

Step 2

◆ Pray 2 rak'at as a greeting of the mosque.

COMMENTS

◆ Always have the intention of following the Sunnah of Prophet Muhammad (pbuh).

WARNING: *There are no rituals for visiting this mosque.*

"مَن تطهرَ في بيته وأتى إلى مسجدِ قباء وصلى ركعتين ،
فله أجرُ عمرةٍ ."
أخرجه الترمذي.

Quba' Mosque

This is the first mosque in Islam.

NEXT STEP: Return home safely.

Supplications

Supplication (Du'a') is truly the essence of sincere worship. It connects Muslims with their Creator and it is a practical expression of their persisting need for Almighty Allah.

Almighty Allah asks people to be persistent in their du'a' and never to lose hope in beseeching Him and Him alone. Who else except Allah would respond to our supplication and du'a'? He Himself said: "And if My servants ask you about me-behold-I am near; I respond to the call of them who call, whenever they call upon Me." So let them also listen to Me and believe in Me, in order that they may be guided to the right way." (2: 186).

In another verse Allah urges people to make du'a': "Your Lord said: If you beseach Me I will respond to you." (40: 60)

However, for du'a' to be accepted and responded to, a Muslim must be truthful, with true intention, clean and pure heart, humble, legitimate in earning money, and should avoid over-indulgence in worldly matters.

The best type of du'a' is one that is mentioned in the Qur'an and the Sunnah of Prophet Muhammad (peace be upon him).

Here are some supplications, taken from the Holy Qur'an and the Prophet's Sunnah (pbuh). These supplications can be used whenever du'a' is permissible.

Yaarabbi! laka-l-hamdu kamaa yanbaghii lijalaali wajhika wa ʿaẓiimi sultaanika.

يَارَبِّ لَكَ الحمدُ كما يَنبغي لجلالِ وجهكَ ولعظيمِ سلطانكَ.

Oh Lord! Yours is the Praise that befits the Glory of Your Face and the Might of Your Dominion.

Rabbanaa laka-l-hamdu mil^assamaawaati wal-ardi wa mil^a maa shi^ta min shay^in baʿd, ahla-tthanaa^i wal-majd.

رَبَّنا لكَ الحمدُ مِلءَ السماواتِ والأرضِ وملءَ ما شِئتَ مِنْ شيءٍ بعد، أهلَ الثناءِ والمجد.

O our Lord! Yours is the Praise that fills the heavens, the earth, and whatever you will thereafter. You are worthy of Praise and Glory.

Allahumma ^nnaka ʿafuwwun kariimun tuhibbu-l'afwa fa'fu ʿannii.

اللَّهُمَّ إنكَ عفوٌ كريمٌ تحبُّ العفوَ فاعفُ عَنِي.

O Allah! You are oft-forgiving, oft-generous, and forgiveness loving. So Forgive me!

Allahumma yaa musarrifa-l-quluubi ṣarrif quluubanaa ʿalaa taa'atika.

اللَّهُمَّ يامُصَرِّفَ القُلوبِ صَرِّفْ قلوبَنا على طاعَتِكَ.

O Allah! Changer of hearts! Drive our hearts toward Your obedience!

Allahumma yaa muqalliba-l-quluubi thabbit quluubanaa ʿalaa diinika.

اللَّهُمَّ يا مُقَلِّبَ القلوبِ ثَبَتْ قُلوبَنا على دينَكَ.

O Allah! Changer of hearts! Establish our hearts on Your Religion!

Allahumma ^nnii ^as^aluka ʿilman naafi'an wa qalban khaashi'an wa yaqiinan saadiqan wa lisaanan ẓaakiran.

اللَّهُمَّ إني أسأُلكَ عِلماً نافعاً، وقَلباً خاشعاً، ويقيناً صادقاً، ولساناً ذاكراً.

O Allah! I ask You for a beneficial knowledge, a submitting heart, a sincere conviction and an invoking tongue.

Allahumma-j'ali-l-qur^aana rabii'a qalbii wa nuura baṣarii wa jalaa^a huznii wa zahaaba hammii.

اللَّهُمَّ اجعلِ القرآنَ رَبيعَ قَلبي ونورَ بَصَري وجَلاءَ حُزني وذهابَ هَمِّي.

O Allah! Let the Qur'an be the springtime of my heart, the light of my sight, the cleanser of my sorrow and the remover of my care!

Rabbanaa ^aatinaa fi-ddunyaa hasanatan wa fi-^aakhirati hasanatan wa qinaa ʿaẓaaba-nnaar.

رَبَّنا آتِنا في الدُّنيا حَسنةً وفي الآخِرةِ حَسنةً وقِنا عَذابَ النارِ.

O our Lord! Grant unto us a reward in this life, a reward in the afterlife, and protect us from the chastisement in the Hellfire!

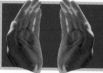

Supplications

Allahumma ^nnii ^as^aluka-l-khayra kullahu 'aajilahu wa ^aajilahu wa ^'uuzu bika mina-shsharri kullihi 'aajilihi wa ^aajilihi.

اللّٰهُمَّ إني أسألُكَ الخَيرَ كُلَّهُ: عاجِلَهُ وآجِلَهُ وأعوذُ بكَ من الشَّرِّ كلِّه: عاجلِه وآجلِه.

O Allah! I ask You for all the good, in the present and in the future, and I take refuge in You from all evil, in the present and in the future.

Allahumma ^nnii ^as^aluka ridaaka wa—jannata wa 'uuzu bika min sakhatika wa-nnaar.

اللّٰهُمَّ إني أسألكَ رِضاكَ والجنةَ، وأعوذُ بكَ من سَخَطِكَ والنارِ.

O Allah! I ask You for Your Pleasure and Heaven, and I take refuge in You from Your Displeasure and the Hellfire.

Allahumma ^a'innii 'alaa zikrika wa shukrika wa husni 'ibaadatika.

اللّٰهُمَّ أعِني على ذِكرِكَ، وشُكرِكَ، وحُسنِ عِبادتكَ

O Allah! Help me to invoke You, to be grateful to You and to worship You well.

Rabbanaa hab lanaa min ^azwaajinaa wa zurriyyaatinaa qurrata ^a'yunin waj'alnaa lilmuttaqiina ^imaaman.

رَبَّنا هَبْ لنا من أزواجِنا وذرياتِنا قُرَّةَ أعيُنٍ واجعَلنا للمُتَّقينَ إماماً.

O our Lord! Grant unto us delight and pleasure in our spouses and offspring, and let us be a leader to the righteous!

Allahumma ^nnii ^as^aluka-l-hudaa wa-ttuqaa wa-l-'afaafa wa-l-ghinaa.

اللّٰهُمَّ إني أسألُكَ الهُدَىَ والتُّقَىَ والعَفَافَ والغِنَىَ.

O Allah! I ask You for guidance, righteousness, modesty and wealth.

Rabbanaa 'alayka tawakkalnaa wa ^ilayka ^anabnaa wa ^ilayka-l-masiir.

رَبَّنا عَليكَ تَوَكَّلنا وإليكَ أنبنا وإليكَ المَصيرِ.

O our Lord! On You we depend, to You we repent, and onto You we return.

Allahumma habbib ^ilayna-l-^iimana wa zayyinhu fi quluubinaa wa karrih ^ilayna-l-kufra wa-l-fusuuqa wa-l-'isyaan.

اللّٰهُمَّ حَبِّبْ إلينا الإيمانَ وزَينهُ في قُلوبِنا وكَرِّه إلينا الكُفرَ والفُسُوقَ والعِصيانَ.

O Allah! Endear the Faith to us and beautify it in our hearts, and make us hate unbelief, sinning and rebellion!

Rabbanaa laa tuzigh quluubanaa ba'da ^iz hadaytanaa wa hab lanaa min ladunka rahmatan ^innaka ^anta-l-wahhaab.

رَبَّنا لا تُزِغْ قلوبنا بعد إذ هديتنا وهبْ لنا من لدنكَ رحمةً إنك أنت الوهاب.

O our Lord! Do not let our hearts stray after You have guided us, and grant unto us Mercy from You! You verily are the oft-Grantor.

Rabbana-ghfir lanaa zunuubanaa wa ^israafanaa fii ^amrinaa wa thabbit ^aqdaamanaa
wanṣurnaa 'ala-l-qawmi-l-kaafiriin.

رَبَّنَا اغفِرْ لنا ذُنوبَنا وإسرافَنا في أمرِنا وثَبتْ أقدامَنا وانصرنا على القومِ الكافرينَ.

O our Lord! Forgive our sins and our indulgence, and let us gain foothold,
and grant unto us victory over the unbelievers!

Rabbana-ghfir lii wa liwaalidayya wa lilmu^miniina yawma yaquumu-l-hisaab.

رَبَّنا اغفِر لي ولوالِدَّي وللمؤمنينَ يومَ يقومُ الحسابُ.

O our Lord! Forgive me, my parents, and all believers on the Day of Judgment!

Allahumma ^anta-ssalaamu wa minka-ssalaamu fa hayyinaa bissalaam.

اللَّهُمَّ أنتَ السَّلامُ ومِنكَ السَّلامُ فحيِنا رَبنا بالسَّلامِ.

O Allah! Peace You are and from You come Peace, so greet us with Peace!

A'uuzu billaahi-l-'aẓiimi wa biwajhihi-l-kariimi wa sultaanihi-l-qadiimi mina-shshaytaani-rrajiim.

أعوذ بالله العظيمِ، وبوجهِه الكَريمِ، وسلطانِه القَديمِ، من الشيَطانِ الرَّجيمِ.

I take refuge in the Almighty Allah, in His Beneficent Face, and in His eternal
Dominion from the outcast Satan.

Allahumma-ghfir wa-rham wa-'fu 'amma ta'lam wa ^anta-l-^a'azzu-l-^akram.

اللَّهُمَّ اغفِرْ وارْحم واعفُ عما تعلمُ وأنتَ الأعزُ الأكرمُ.

O Allah! Forgive, grant mercy, and excuse that which You know (of me)!
You are the Almighty, the All-generous.

Allahumma ^nnii ^as^aluka 'ilman naafi'an wa rizqan waasi'an wa shifaa^an min kulli daa^.

اللَّهُمَّ إني أسألكَ علماً نافعاً ورزقاً واسعاً وشفاءً من كُلِّ داءٍ.

O Allah! I ask You for a beneficial knowledge, a gracious sustenance, and a healing from every ailment.

اللَّهُمَّ صَلِ عَلَى محمَّدٍ وعَلى آلِ محمَّدٍ كَما صَلَّيت على إبراهيمَ وعلى آلِ إبراهيم

وبارِكْ على محمَّدٍ وعِلى آلِ محمَّدٍ كَما بارَكتَ عَلى إبراهيمَ وعلى آلِ إبراهيم

Glossary

Al-Haram:	The holy city of Makkah.
Al-Mash'ar Al-Haraam:	The valley between Muzdalifah and Mina, where pilgrims should make du'a' after they have slept in Muzdalifah while they are going to Makkah to throw Jamrat Al-Aqabah on the morning of the 10th of Dhul-Hijjah.
Al-Masjid Al-Haraam:	The mosque where the Ka'bah is located, in Makkah, in western Saudi Arabia.
'Arafat ('Arafah):	The area that surrounds Mount Rahmah, southeast of Makkah.
At-tahallul Al-Asghar:	The partial ending of the state of Ihram, which allows the pilgrim to practice normal life, except for sexual intercourse.
At-tahallul Al-Akbar:	The total ending of the state of Ihram, which lifts all the obligations from the pilgrim and allows him/her to practice normal life.
Du'a':	Supplication to Allah.
Ghusl:	Taking a shower/bath with the intention to purify oneself.
Hajj:	The 5th pillar of Islam, to be performed at least once in one's lifetime.
Hijr Isma'il:	The semi-circular short wall, located a few meters east of the Ka'bah and considered part of the Ka'bah. Therefore, the pilgrim should go around it while making Tawaf.
Ifadah:	Refers to the Tawaf that is done by a Muslim when he/she comes from Muzdalifah.
Ifrad:	The type of Hajj where a pilgrim makes only Hajj, without making 'Umrah (see types of Hajj).
Ihram:	The state in which one starts 'Umrah or Hajj, and during which certain acts are prohibited.
Jamarat:	The three stone pillars at which pilgrims throw pebbles.
Jamarat al-'Aqabah:	The closest stone pillar to Makkah, also known as Al Jamarah al-Kubra.
Ka'bah:	The square stone building in Al-Haraam mosque in Makkah and towards which all Muslims face in every prayer.
Madinah:	The city to which Prophet Muhammad (peace be upon him) migrated, about 450 Km northeast of Makkah.
Makkah:	The holiest city for Muslims, located in western Saudi Arabia.
Mahram:	A wife's husband or any escort relative who is not legitimately permitted to marry her, such as grandfather, father, uncle, brother, son.
Masjid Quba':	The first mosque in Islam. It is 5km from al-Masjid al-Haram.

Glossary

Maqam Ibrahim: Abraham's Station, a small glass station 30 feet from the Ka'bah door. It is the place where Prophet Abraham used to stand when he was building the Ka'bah.

Marwah: The hill on which a pilgrim ends his/her sa'ee . It is 250m northeast of the Ka'bah.

Mina: An area close to Makkah on the road to 'Arafah.

Miqat: The place where Muslims declare their intentions to make Hajj or 'Umrah and begin the state of Ihram. There are only 5 miqat locations: Dhul-Hulaifah from the north, Dhat I'rq and Qarn Al-Manazil from the east, Yalamlam from the south, and Rabigh from the northwest.

Muzdalifah: The place between A'rafah and Mina where pilgrims stay the night on the 10th of Dhul-Hijjah.

Safa: The hill on which a pilgrim begins his/her sa'ee (walking). It is about 200 m southeast of the Ka'bah.

Sa'ee: The act of walking between the two hills - Safa and Marwah.

Shirk: Associating others with Allah.

Takbeer: Saying " Allahu Akbar" (Allah is great).

Talbiyah: The response to Allah's call for Hajj.

Tamattu': The type of Hajj where a pilgrim starts with 'Umrah then makes the Hajj later on but in the same year.

Tarwiyah: The 8th day of Dhul-Hijjah.

Tashreeq: The 11th, 12th, and 13th of Dhul-Hijjah.

Tawaf: Circling the Ka'bah.

The Black Stone: The stone in the southeast corner of the Ka'bah from which Muslims begin the Tawaf.

Dhikr: Mentioning Allah, as in du'a' or reciting verses of the Qur'an.

'Umrah: An Islamic ritual that is performed at Makkah anytime of the year. It includes Tawaf 7 times around the Ka'bah and walking 7 times between the hills of Safa and Marwah. It also requires some obligations from the pilgrim until the state of Ihram is ended.

Qiran: The type of Hajj where a pilgrim makes 'Umrah in the same state of Ihram.

Zamzam: The name of the well of water that sprang up beneath Prophet Isma'il when he was an infant. It is about 150 m southeast of the Ka'bah.

Al-Bukhari, Muhammad I. (1981). *Sahih Al-Bukhari.* Beirut, Lebanon: Dar Al-Fikr.

Al-Fouzan, Sale<u>h</u> F. (1994). *Explanation of What a Pilgrim and a Muslim Performing 'Umrah Should Do.* Riyadh, Saudi Arabia: Imam Muhammad ibn Saud Islamic University.

'Ali, Abdullah Yusuf (1992). *The Meaning of the Holy Qur'an.* Brentwood, Maryland: Amana Corporation.

Al-Jasim, Yasin (1987). *Al-Minhaj lil Mútamir Wal Hajj.* Kuwait; Dar Ad-dawah.

Al-Khatib, Mu<u>h</u>ammad A. (1993). *Pilgrimage: A Divine Camp.* Cairo, Egypt: Dar Al-Manar Al-<u>H</u>aditha.

'Al-Khen, M., Al-Bugha, M., & Al-Sharbaji, A. (1987). *Al-Fiqh Al-Manhaji.* Damascus, Syria: Dar al-Qalam.

Al-Mahrouk, Abdul Fatta<u>h</u> (1988). *Supplication.* Mansurah, Egypt : Dar Al-Wafa'.

An-Naisabury, Muslim H. (1929). *Sahih Muslim.* Cairo, Egypt: Egyptian Press, Al-Azhar.

At-Tayyar, Abdullah (1993). *The <u>H</u>ajj.* Riyadh, Saudi Arabia: Imam Muhammad ibn Saud Islamic University.

Al-'Utaibi, Ala' ed-deen (1993). *Supplication of Day and Night.* Riyadh, Saudi Arabia: Al-Mu'tamin Corporation.

Al-Zuhaily, Wahbah (1989). *Islamic Fiqh and its Proofs.* Damascus, Syria: Dar Al-Fikr.

Husain, Ibrahim (1977). *Handbook of <u>H</u>ajj.* Indianapolis, Indiana : Islamic Teaching Center.

Ibn Baz, 'Abdul Aziz, A (1993). *Important Fatwas Regarding the Rites of <u>H</u>ajj and 'Umrah.* Riyadh, Saudi Arabia.

Ibn Baz, 'Abdul Aziz A. (1991). *How the Messenger (pbuh) Performed <u>H</u>ajj.* Riyadh, Saudi Arabia: Dar As-Salam.

Peters, E. (1994). *The <u>H</u>ajj: The Muslim Pilgrimage to Mecca and the Holy Places.* Princeton, New Jersey: Princeton University press.

Pickthall, Mohammed M. (1990). *The Meaning of the Glorious Koran.* New York: Penguin Group.

_____(1993). *A Guide to <u>H</u>ajj, 'Umrah, and Visiting the Prophet's Mosque.* Riyadh, Saudi Arabia: The Cooperative Office for Call and Guidance.

_____(1993). *The Rationale of <u>H</u>ajj.* Jakarta, Indonesia: The Department of Religious Affairs .

_____(1989). *Understanding Islam and the Muslims.* Washington DC: The Saudi Embassy.

Yamani, Muhammed 'Abduh (1994). *How the Messenger of Allah Performed <u>H</u>ajj.* Jeddah, Saudi Arabia: The Saudi Company for Research and Publication.

Hajj Rituals Day by Day

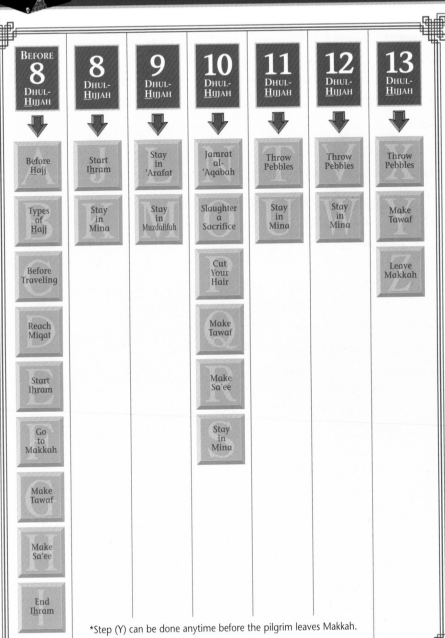

BEFORE 8 DHUL-HIJJAH	8 DHUL-HIJJAH	9 DHUL-HIJJAH	10 DHUL-HIJJAH	11 DHUL-HIJJAH	12 DHUL-HIJJAH	13 DHUL-HIJJAH
Before Hajj	Start Ihram	Stay in 'Arafat	Jamrat al-'Aqabah	Throw Pebbles	Throw Pebbles	Throw Pebbles
Types of Hajj	Stay in Mina	Stay in Muzdalifah	Slaughter a Sacrifice	Stay in Mina	Stay in Mina	Make Tawaf
Before Traveling			Cut Your Hair			Leave Makkah
Reach Miqat			Make Tawaf			
Start Ihram			Make Sa'ee			
Go to Makkah			Stay in Mina			
Make Tawaf						
Make Sa'ee						
End Ihram						

*Step (Y) can be done anytime before the pilgrim leaves Makkah.

ORDER FORM

YES, I want to buy _____ copy(s) _Hajj & Umrah from A to Z._ **Book** (ISBN 0-9652877-0-x)

By: Dr. Mamdouh N. Mohamed
Each book is: $12.50 + $4.00 for S & H

Make Checks payable to:

B 200 Inc.
2831 Gallows Rd. Suite 251 • Falls Church, VA 22042 USA

If you want to order by credit cards visit our website at
www.islamfromAtoZ.com

Name:_____

Address:_____

City/State/ Zip:_____

Phone:_____

E-mail:_____

ORDER FORM

YES, I want to buy _____ copy(s) _Salaat: The Islamic Prayer from A to Z._ **Package** (ISBN 0-9652877-2-6)

By: Dr. Mamdouh N. Mohamed
Each book is: $29.95 + $4.00 for S & H

Make Checks payable to:

B 200 Inc.
2831 Gallows Rd. Suite 251 • Falls Church, VA 22042 USA

If you want to order by credit cards visit our website at
www.islamfromAtoZ.com

Name:_____

Address:_____

City/State/ Zip:_____

Phone:_____

E-mail:_____

Before embarking
on your <u>H</u>ajj see how
others evaluated their experience.

www.HajjRatings.com

Upon returning,
rate your journey
from A to Z.

About the Author

Dr. Mamdouh N. Mohamed

Professor at Johns Hopkins, George Mason University & The American Open University

He was born in Egypt 1949.

He received both his Masters and Ph. D. from George Mason University, USA.

He has worked as a teacher and teacher-trainer for more than 30 years.

He is an instructional technologist.

His most famous works are:

Salaat from A to Z
Arabic for Children
Mission Survival
The Religion of Islam
Arabic: A Bridge to Islamic Culture

He is a co-founder of 5 educational institutions worldwide.

He received a patent in computer design from the USA Patent Office.

e-mail address:
info@arabicforeveryone.com

1-800
732

9966

for shop
insur.

colorup